WordPress Securit

for Webmaster 2021

How to Stop Hackers Breaking into Your Website

Dr. Andy Williams

Updated: 16th February 2021

What people are saying about previous versions of this book:

"Andy's advice in this book is as objective, practical, and pragmatic as any you'll ever come across. Andy always speaks from pure experience. His narratives are invaluable, unselfish, and indispensable." **Amazon Customer**

"Good read. Useful, actionable information." **Howard Lee Harkness**

"Everyone using WordPress needs to read and follow this book... Step by step, you are instructed on how to add protection to tour site." **Thomas Bogan**

"Easy to understand book on WordPress Security. Excellent! Dr. Andy Williams does it again! I'm a huge fan of his books. He always over-delivers and makes the most complicated subjects understandable." **Carol Youmans**

"Dr. Andy Williams always does a good job. He puts everything in his work. All the details are specifically mentioned, and no stone left unturned." **Evelyn Guzman**

"It is great. Easy to understand. Thanks, Andy." **Tin**

"Awesome. This comprehensive guide covers everything you didn't know you didn't know about WordPress security (if you're a beginner with WordPress) and is explained so easily and step-by-step; this has been a life saver for me! Thanks, Andy." **Megan**

Contents

DISCLAIMER AND TERMS OF USE AGREEMENT

A Little History

In the early days, websites were hand-built using a special code called HyperText Markup Language (HTML). To create good-looking websites back then, you had to be something of a geek. Then, special tools came onto the market to reduce the learning curve associated with building websites in HTML. Two of the more popular ones were Macromedia Dreamweaver (now owned by Adobe) and Microsoft Front Page (discontinued in 2006). The problem with these web development tools is that they were expensive.

In May 2003, Matt Mullenweg & Mike Little released a new tool that would change the face of website building forever. They called it WordPress.

I have to admit I was a little reluctant to give up my copy of Dreamweaver at first. But in 2004, I began to experiment with the WordPress platform. It was a time when WordPress was just starting to get interesting. This was thanks to the introduction of something we now know as "plugins."

Fast-forward to today, and WordPress is now the site-building tool of choice. It's popular with professionals and enthusiasts alike. Home-based businesses run by moms & dads love it, as do school kids running blogs about their favorite bands or video games. Today, even large corporations use WordPress and just about everyone else who builds websites.

WordPress is extremely powerful, flexible, and produces very professional-looking websites and blogs. It's pretty easy to use too, but best of all is that it's 100% free.

The other advantage of WordPress is that the code is freely available to anyone who needs it. This same advantage, though, is also its biggest security threat. The open nature of the code means developers can create exciting new plugins and themes to extend the functionality. Alas, it also means hackers can find security holes in the code and use them to gain illegal access to WordPress websites.

A lot of the discussion on website security can get overly technical. Even so, the average webmaster needs to be able to protect and secure their website. That means there should be no technical barriers to stop the average user. It's why we need these things written in plain and simple English.

That's where this book comes in.

I'm going to take you by the hand and guide you — one easy step at a time — as you secure your website(s) against hackers.

How to Use This Book

I wrote this book for anyone who runs a WordPress website. I won't assume you have any technical knowledge at all. You don't have to worry about steep learning curves or technical skill requirements. There aren't any.

What you have here is a hands-on tutorial. To get the most out of it, I recommend you sit at your computer and follow the steps outlined in these pages. Whenever I do something on my demo site, you do the same on your site. Don't be afraid to make mistakes, as they can easily be undone.

There are two main sections in the book.

The first section looks at the various ways hackers can gain access to your site and how you can STOP them. I also provide detailed instructions on ways to plug these security holes. Don't worry; you don't need to do anything at this point, not if you don't want to.

The second part of the book covers a comprehensive security plugin. This plugin secures your site using a simple point-and-click interface. You'll learn about website security in the very first section of the book. You then just follow my lead as we set up the plugin to secure your site against hackers.

By the end of this book, you'll have a solid understanding of WordPress security. You'll also know the measures to take to secure your website(s).

I have good news for anyone who likes to learn via audio-visual. You should find my companion WordPress Security video course very interesting. There are around 2.5 hours of video tuition and a Q&A section where you can ask me questions. You can find details in the Resources section at the end of this book.

A Note About UK v US English

There are some differences between UK and US English. While I try to be consistent, some errors may slip into my writing because I spend a lot of time corresponding with people in both the UK and the US. The line can blur.

Examples of this include the spelling of words like optimise (UK) v optimize (US).

The difference I get the most complaints about is with collective nouns. Collective nouns refer to a group of individuals, e.g., Google. In the US, collective nouns are singular, so **Google IS** a company. However, in the UK, collective nouns are usually plural, so **Google ARE** a company. This is not to be confused with Google, "the search engine," which is singular in both.

There are other differences too. I hope that if I have been inconsistent anywhere in this book, it does not detract from the value you get from it.

WordPress itself will have some differences depending on whether you are using UK or US

English. The one I find most obvious is in the labeling of the area containing things you have deleted.

If you installed WordPress with US English, you'd see this called "trash":

Comments

All (1) | Pending (0) | Approved (1) | Spam (0) | Trash (0)

But if your WordPress is installed with UK English, this becomes "bin":

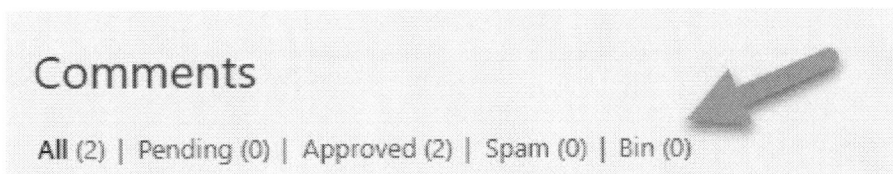

Comments

All (2) | Pending (0) | Approved (2) | Spam (0) | Bin (0)

There are other places in the dashboard that use localized words like this. I'll leave those for you to find.

Found Typos in This Book?

Errors can get through proof-readers, so if you do find any typos or grammatical errors in this book, I'd be very grateful if you could let me know using this email address:

typos@ezseonews.com

SECTION 1 - About Security & Hacking

The first section of the book outlines the main ways a hacker will try to gain access to your site. It also looks at how you can prevent these things from happening.

Chapter 1 – Introduction

In 2018, a report by infosecurity-magazine.com suggested that WordPress accounted for 90% of all hacked sites, up from 83% in 2017. WordPress is a target for hackers because of its huge user-base. Fortunately for you, WordPress's "core" is very secure. Unfortunately for you, hackers find their way into sites because of mistakes made by site administrators and security holes in third-party addons like plugins and themes. One report I read suggested that 98% of WordPress vulnerabilities are related to plugins. Another, more conservative report suggested that figure was 52%, but it's still a large number. Another statistic showed that 8% of WordPress websites were hacked because of weak passwords. According to Sucuri, 61% of infected WordPress sites are out of date. WordFence, a company specializing in WordPress security, said there were 90,000 attacks per minute on WordPress websites.

Hackers hack websites for a variety of purposes. Some will want to redirect your traffic. Hackers also attempt to steal customer details, delete files, or change your login details to lock you out. Some will send spam emails to millions of people, SEO for the hacker's site, and other, more sinister reasons.

Don't think that your small, insignificant site is safe from hackers—it's not. To a hacker, a site is a site, and they'll attack it if it serves their purpose. They use computer software to auto-scan millions of websites for vulnerabilities. Once found, they'll attack any soft targets they come across. There is no softer target than a newly setup WordPress website run from a bedroom.

There are good reasons to worry about your website security. Despite the scare, I don't want you to avoid WordPress thinking it's an insecure platform. As I've already said, it isn't. When the WordPress security team finds a security hole, they usually plug it fast. They then automatically push the update out to all WordPress installs.

The real security issues derive from the folks who run the websites. They often don't have the knowledge to make the best-informed decisions. They don't know enough about content, the plugins they use, or the themes they install.

This book has two aims:

1. I want to give you the knowledge you need so you can understand where the main threats come from. With this knowledge, you'll understand how your administrative actions can affect the security of your website. Your new understanding then gives you the power to stop hackers.

2. I want to give you a step-by-step solution to make your website as hackproof as possible. We'll install an excellent WordPress plugin and go through the entire setup process. For your part, just follow along on your site as I secure one of my own.

If you're not technically minded, don't worry. This book assumes no technical ability and no programming skills.

Chapter 2 – Why Do Hackers Hack

I guess you want something a little more than *because they can,* right?

Unfortunately, this is the reason for a large number of hacking attempts these days. Hackers often leave behind a calling card to show how clever they are. It's often in the form of a banner announcing their uninvited presence on your site. It's a kind of virtual ego trip.

Hackers can cause all kinds of damage to your site.

They might delete your content just for laughs. Others "silently" insert malicious code into a site to carry out some dastardly plan. The webmaster doesn't usually get any visual clues to show that someone has compromised their beloved site.

Hacking causes chaos to the site owner and is often time-consuming and expensive to clean up. Some of the more common reasons why hacker's hack include:

1. To break into a popular site to stage some kind of protest.

2. To post banners or extremist messages to support their cause.

3. To insert malware that auto-downloads to the computers of those who visit the pages. This malware can cause all kinds of chaos. They can use it to steal personal data (like credit card details) from the computers it infects.

4. To send huge volumes of spam emails from your domain. This action is likely to get your site closed down by your web host. It's not your fault that millions upon millions of spammy emails leave your server over a short space of time. Despite this, your site cannot be live until you resolve the problem.

5. To gain a competitive advantage. They may embed links into your pages for their SEO purposes. They might also do it to destroy the SEO of the target site so that it drops out of Google's search engine results pages (SERPs).

The bad news is that no amount of security on any site can guarantee it'll be 100% hacker-proof. It all depends on the motivation and resources of the hackers involved. You may have seen recent news reports on some very major hacks. Here are some high-profile hacks.

1. In July 2019, online bank Capitol One found out that its data had been hacked. Sensitive information on hundreds of thousands of credit card applications, like birthdates and social security numbers, was exposed. This attack was done by an American named Paige Thompson, who knew that Capitol One's Amazon AWS server was badly configured because she had previously worked at Amazon.

2. In April 2019, the Weather Channel became the victim of a ransomware attack. The service was offline for nearly 90 minutes. Fortunately, the Weather Channel didn't need to pay over the Bitcoin ransom as they had good backups and reinstated their service within 2 hours.

3. In May 2019, U.S. Customs and Border Protection was the target of a cyberattack.

Images of people's faces (used in the facial recognition program and license plates were exposed. Information found its way onto the Dark Web. It was ironic that the agency dedicated to protecting US borders couldn't protect its data.

4. In August 2019, 22 small Texas towns were hit by ransomware attacks leaving the government paralyzed, unable to provide basic services. The towns refused to pay the millions in ransom, but thanks to remediation efforts, they were back up and running in a matter of weeks.

These are just a few of the high-profile cyber-attacks that have happened in recent months on large Corporations.

Fortunately, when dealing with WordPress, there are simple measures you can take to make your site as hack-proof as possible. There are other measures you can take to ensure you never lose your site or your website data.

I can promise you that once you've finished this book, your site will be a lot more secure than most other WordPress websites. The type of hacker that's usually responsible for hacking an average website is not going to have the time, patience, or resources to break into yours. Remember, most of these guys look for "soft targets."

There are two sections to this book. You can treat the first one as information-only if you like. I show you some manual procedures for securing against hackers in this section. However, you don't need to do anything as you read the first part. The second section covers a WordPress plugin that secures against all the important threats. This is where I show you the step-by-step instructions on how to install it and set it up to secure your site.

Chapter 3 - WordPress Is Secure, But...

WordPress has a bad reputation when it comes to security, but that reputation is wrong. It's true; WordPress websites do tend to get hacked a lot. Remember, 90% of all hacked websites run on WordPress. However, these hacks are usually because of the webmaster and not WordPress itself.

WordPress is open source. That means the programming code behind it is free for anyone to look at and modify if they so wish. They created WordPress this way so that third-party developers could extend its features. That meant anyone could create and distribute new WordPress themes and plugins.

The freedom to offer WordPress enhancements is enough to start alarm bells ringing. Imagine a hacker who wanted to infiltrate a lot of websites. What better way than to develop a really useful plugin or a cool theme and offer them for free? Can you see the problem?

Plugins and themes represent one of the top three ways to hack a WordPress website. If the plugin or theme is not in itself malicious, it could still have vulnerabilities in its code. Any weaknesses can provide a doorway to hackers.

The good news is that WordPress runs "repositories" for themes and plugins. WordPress.org carefully vets any plugin or theme included in these repositories. This safeguard is to ensure they don't contain any vulnerabilities or malicious code. So the key here is to simply choose plugins and themes from authorized sources. Just by doing this, you already take a giant step to secure your site against hackers.

So, plugins & themes are one of the top three ways for hackers to hack WordPress websites and blogs. Maybe you can guess the other two?

- Weak usernames and passwords
- Not keeping software up to date

Weak usernames and passwords are a common route to a hack. They're a hassle, though, right? After all, we have so many usernames and passwords to remember these days. This includes things like bank details, website logins, utility bill sites, and online shopping stores, etc. It's the reason why a lot of people use the same username and/or password for multiple site logins.

Be warned!

If a hacker gets access to just one of your accounts, they can usually gain access to a lot more by using the same login details.

Think about your passwords.

Do you have them written down in a little book somewhere? What if you lose that book or someone steals it? Do you use the same password for multiple online accounts? Is it a "secure" password? It's a good question, bearing in mind that automated software tools can try hundreds of password combinations a second?

We'll go over the dos and don'ts of passwords later in the book.

Not updating software is another very common problem. The software includes things like themes, plugins, and WordPress core files. When the WordPress team finds vulnerabilities, it's usually quick to plug them. If you keep WordPress up to date, hackers cannot use those vulnerabilities to gain access. If you don't keep it up to date, hackers have an easy way into your site.

What makes things even easier for hackers is that WordPress can show them exactly what version you're using. All they have to do then is look up vulnerabilities in that particular version and use them to hack your site.

This all sounds bad, doesn't it? Don't panic!

There's one thing these three major security issues have in common that gives you the upper hand:

THE USER CAUSES THE PROBLEMS, NOT WORDPRESS

As the webmaster, it's what you do (or don't do) to your site that makes it secure or insecure. I say again, WordPress is very secure.

There's a team of 25 experts (researchers and developers) who continually work to make WordPress even more secure. Since version 3.7, automated updates fix all security issues routinely, without you having to lift a finger.

Chapter 4 – Learning What Needs to Be Secured

This chapter takes you through the main security threats. It's where I offer you some advice on what you should be doing to secure your site. In some cases, you can go ahead and make changes as you read through the chapter. In most instances, though, I'll tell you not to worry about doing anything right away. This is because the security plugin we install and configure in the second part of the book will do it all for you.

I've broken the chapter down into "threats." Each "threat" covers a security issue you should know about. Before we start to look at these threats, let's consider the only way to protect your site 100%.

Backup Your Website

The only real way to make your website safe is to back it up. Whatever happens after that, at least you'll always have the files saved to replicate the site again. Even if it means starting over, it's still better than losing everything.

With traditional HTML-based websites, backing up is a simple process. You just copy the files on your hosting server to your computer (download), and that's your full backup. WordPress is a little more complicated, though.

A WordPress website consists of two main parts:

1. The files. This includes the WordPress core files, plugins, themes, and uploaded files like images, and settings.

2. The Database, which stores all your website content.

For a full WordPress website, you need to back up the files AND the database.

There are a lot of tools and plugins available to help you backup your WordPress website. It's important to check what they back up-exactly.

Some only do partial backups like the database. The more useful ones will backup both the database and all the files.

You may think that the only way to do a proper backup is to do a full one. First, you need to be aware of the file size of these backups.

The database-only backups are typically 1-5 MB in size. You can even have these emailed to you.

Full backups can be gigabytes (GB) in size, and they use a lot of server resources to process. Clearly, you cannot receive these by email.

The solution is to use a plugin like UpdraftPlus. There's a free version, which is more than adequate for most users. The premium version is great for anyone who needs more power and options.

UpdraftPlus' free version can automatically backup your site to a remote storage location on a predefined schedule. It includes popular online storage like Dropbox, Google Drive, and Amazon S3, to name a few. If anything should happen to your hosting server, you have offsite backups to fall back on.

To find out more about Updraft, please see:

https://ezseonews.com/updraft

Installing & Setting up UpdraftPlus

As with most trusted plugins, you can find UpdraftPlus in the WordPress repository. You just log in to your WordPress Dashboard and go to "install a new plugin."

Search for "updraft."

As I write this book, you can see the plugin is actively in use by 3+ million websites. It is also updated regularly.

Install and activate Updraft.

Once active, you'll find a new menu under the **Settings** menu, called **UpdraftPlus Backups**.

Clicking on it takes you to a screen showing the current status:

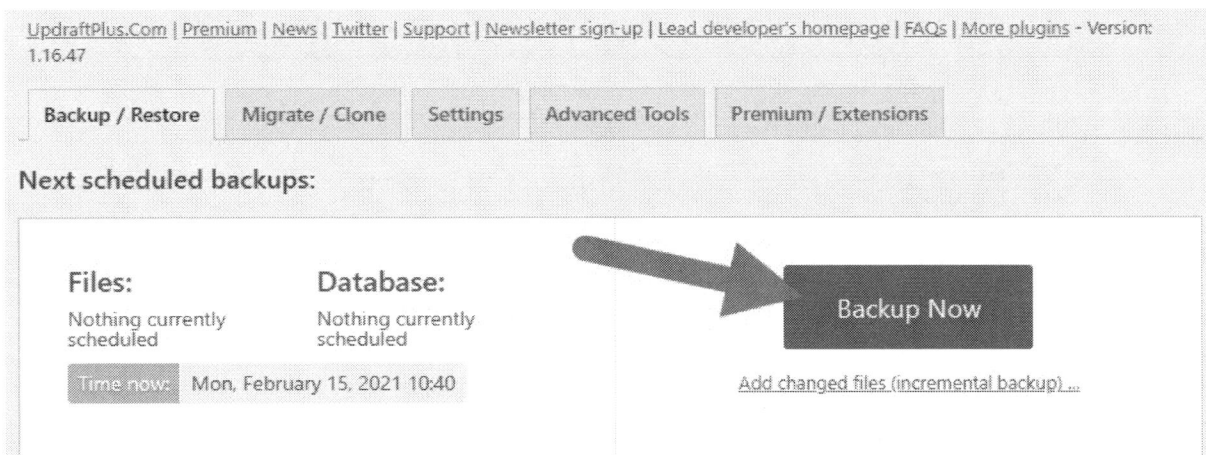

In your case, there won't be any backups yet, but there is a big **Backup Now** button that I recommend you click.

You need to choose what to include in your backup, so choose database and files. You'll notice the disabled box referring to remote storage.

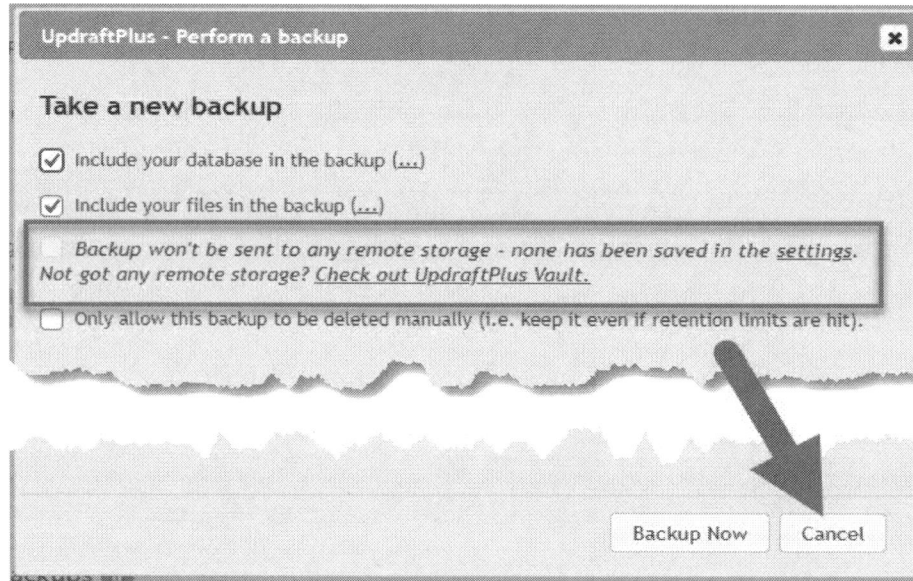

Since we haven't set up remote storage yet, it isn't an option. The program is currently set to store the backup directly on your web server.

However, a backup is not much use if we store it on a hacked server. This is why we need to set up some off-site storage.

OK, now cancel the backup and click on the **Settings** tab.

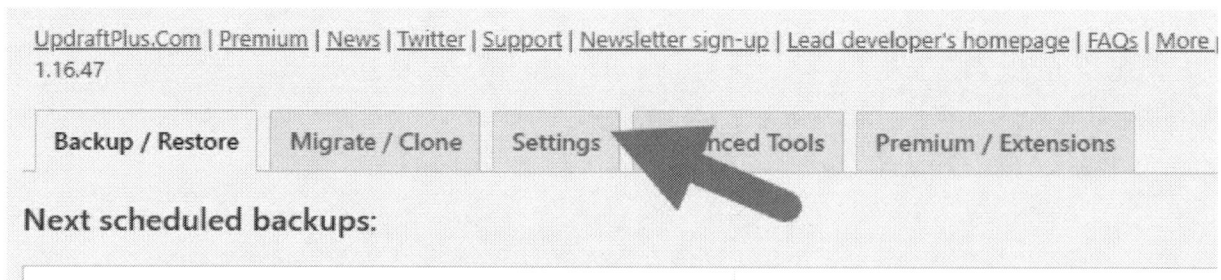

At the top of this screen, you can choose the frequency of automated backups.

The frequency you choose will depend on how often you update your site. If you don't update the site at all, then leave both database and file backups as monthly.

If you update weekly, set the database to weekly but leave the files as monthly.

If you update daily, set the database frequency to at least daily. The file backup frequency is up to you. But remember, it takes more server resources to back up the files. They're also a lot bigger in size, and therefore use more bandwidth when uploading to your off-site storage.

I leave files as monthly for all my sites and then adjust the database, depending on how frequently I update the site.

When you set the frequency, you can also choose how many backups to keep. The only real concern here is how much space you have on your remote storage. I would recommend you always have a minimum of at least three months of backups. Therefore, if backups are monthly, keep 3. If they're weekly, keep 12.

You can now choose the remote storage option.

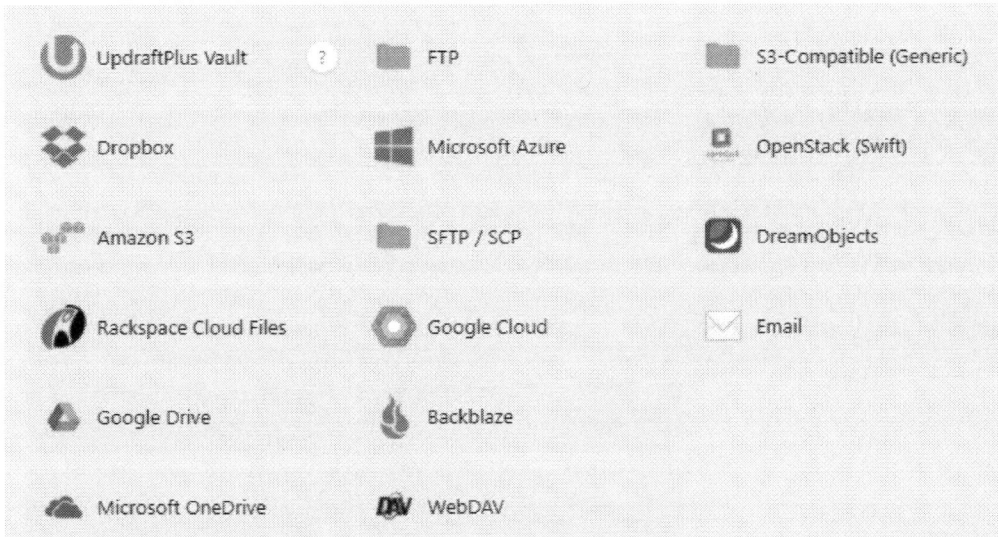

Click your chosen remote storage to select it. I've chosen Dropbox for mine. When you select a remote storage option, more settings will appear on that page related to your choice.

The settings below appeared when I selected Dropbox:

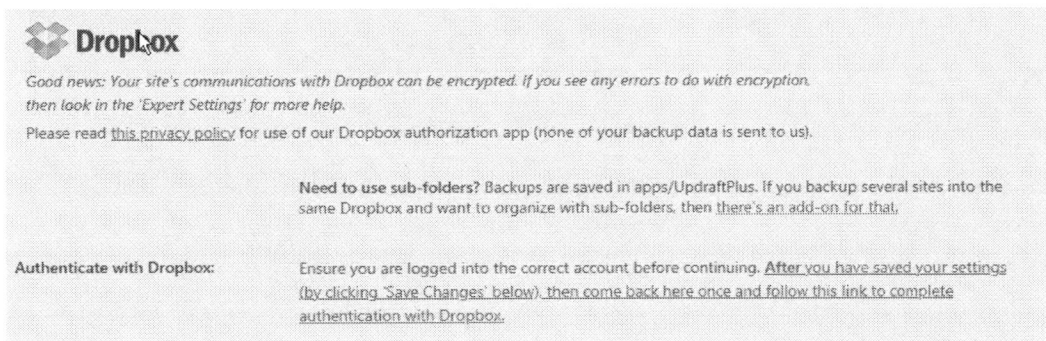

During the process of setting up a storage option, you'll have to authorize UpdraftPlus to log into the chosen site.

You can see the link I need to click to authorize Updraft Plus to use my Dropbox account. Just follow the instructions.

When done, you can continue to scroll down the settings of this plugin. This is where you choose which files to backup and those to exclude—if any:

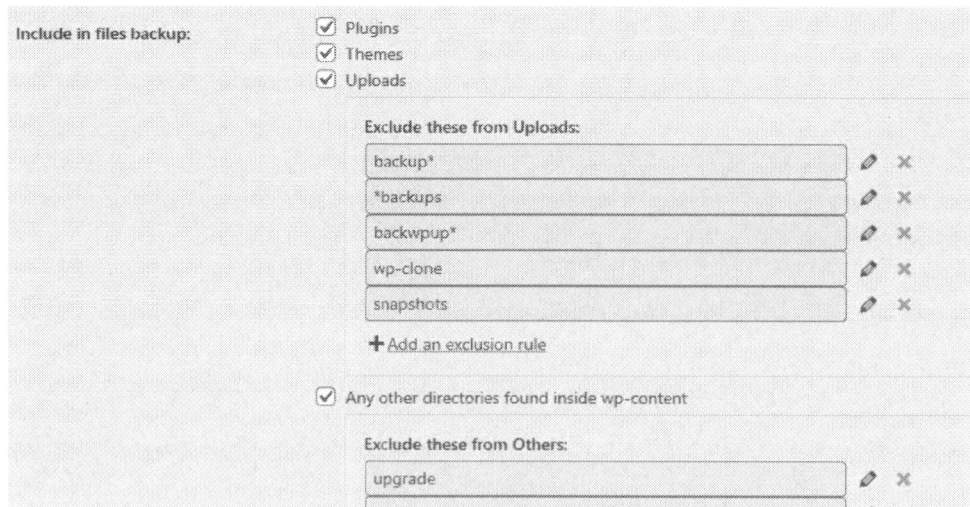

There's also a useful option to have an email report sent with the backup details.

Now click the **save** button at the bottom of the screen. That's all there is to it.

Over on the Backup/Restore tab, you should see a date in the **Next Scheduled Backups** section. This is when the next automated backup will take place.

You can also create a manual backup right now by clicking the **Backup Now** button. You'll then get the option to: **Send this backup to remote storage**:

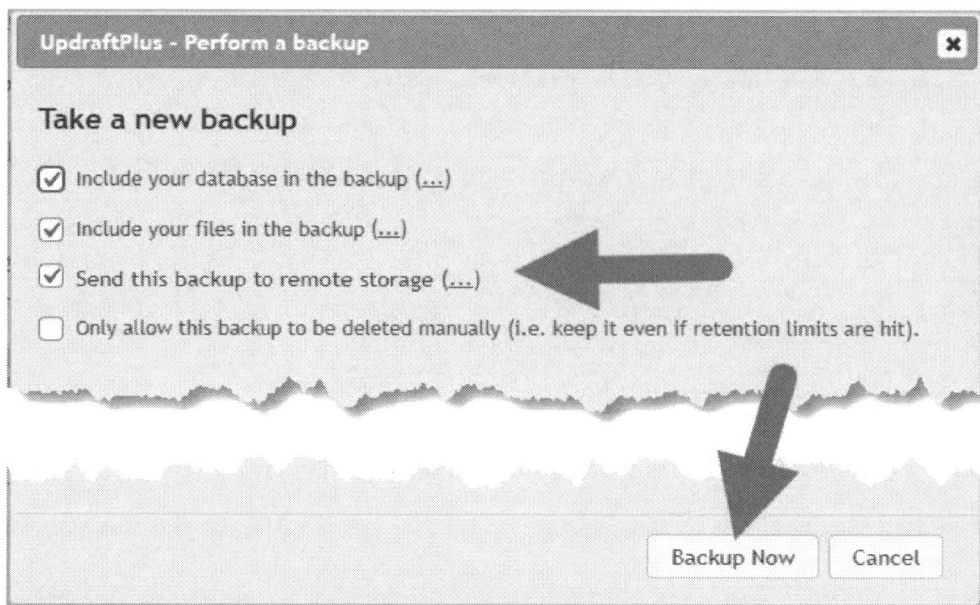

With backups done, you now have everything you need to restore your site to its present glory in any eventuality. It's effectively 100% secure already.

With the site backed up, let's now learn of the threats to your website security.

Threat 1 – Passwords

Earlier in this book, we identified passwords as one of the weakest links in WordPress security.

If you have a strong password, then you have a strong foundation on which to build other security measures. So, what forms a strong password?

There are a few considerations when deciding on a strong password. It should include all the following:

- A random collection of characters
- Include numbers
- Include upper and lower case
- Include special characters

When it comes to passwords, the longer they are, the better.

When they released WordPress 4.3, they introduced strong passwords by default. There is also a tool inside the WordPress Dashboard to generate super secure passwords if you need one. You can find it in your user profile:

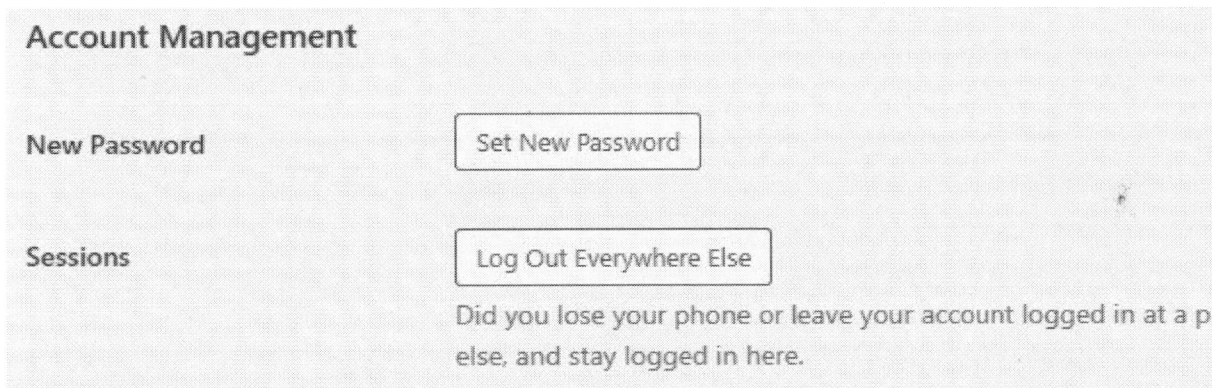

Account Management

New Password   Set New Password

Sessions   Log Out Everywhere Else

Did you lose your phone or leave your account logged in at a pι else, and stay logged in here.

To generate a secure password, click the **Set New Password** button, and WordPress will create one for you:

rxWF#AwPARRI&%83CPQRp5EC   Hide   Cancel

Strong

If you look at the password, you can see it meets the criteria I specified at the start. It's random, includes numbers, upper and lower case, and special characters (#, & and %). It's also a lot longer (24 characters) than the passwords most people make up themselves.

The tool will also give you an idea of how strong your password is. Type it into the box and make sure your password reads **Strong** under the data input field.

I know most people's objections to this type of password.

It's impossible to remember.

That's correct, but there are some great tools out there. These tools not only remember your passwords, but they can also auto-fill them for you as well. I use a tool called Roboform and can highly recommend it. Roboform remembers all my secure passwords (and I have hundreds), and it automatically fills them in for me whenever I visit a website.

NOTE: If you're just installing WordPress, you won't have access to the Dashboard yet, or the password generator tool. Never mind. Do a Google search for **secure password generator** instead. You'll find a few tools which can create these strong, random passwords for you. Lastpass is another popular password manager that provides a free secure password generator. You can get it here:

https://lastpass.com/generatepassword.php

Here are your options with this tool:

Customize your password

Password Length

24

○ Easy to say ⓘ

○ Easy to read ⓘ

◉ All characters ⓘ

☑ Uppercase

☑ Lowercase

☑ Numbers

☑ Symbols

You can choose a 24 character password as WordPress suggests, plus all the other criteria. Here is a sample password generated with that tool:

`tu!YsZPwwh!Gw4PfcptGLMCB`

You can also find free tools online that will check how secure a password is. Here's one example:

HOW SECURE IS MY PASSWORD?

tu!YsZPwwh!Gw4PfcptGLMCB

It would take a computer about

1 OCTILLION YEARS

to crack your password

That's a strong password!

Before you move on in the book, make sure you update your password, if necessary, to make it strong and long.

If you need software to remember passwords, I highly recommend LastPass, which has a good free version:

https://www.lastpass.com/

Threat 2 – WordPress Usernames

Usernames and passwords go together like peanut butter and jelly (that's "jam" in the UK). They're very important as a hacker needs both to log into a website.

Unfortunately, when WordPress installs, it uses the default username **admin.** Most newbies to WordPress don't bother to change it, but they should. By not changing it, you give hackers half of what they need to log into your site!

If you already have your site installed and DID use **admin** as your username, don't panic. When we install the security plugin later, we'll check this and change it if necessary.

When you install WordPress, you can choose your own unique username, and you already know what to do about the password.

Choose a username that is:

- Not easy to guess
- Not **admin**

When I choose a new username, I use the same criteria as for passwords, though maybe only 12-15 characters in length.

Threat 3 - Signing In

When you log into your website, make sure you check the address bar at the top of your browser BEFORE you log in. You should do this check before signing into ANY webpage, whether it's your bank, Paypal, or even your Facebook account.

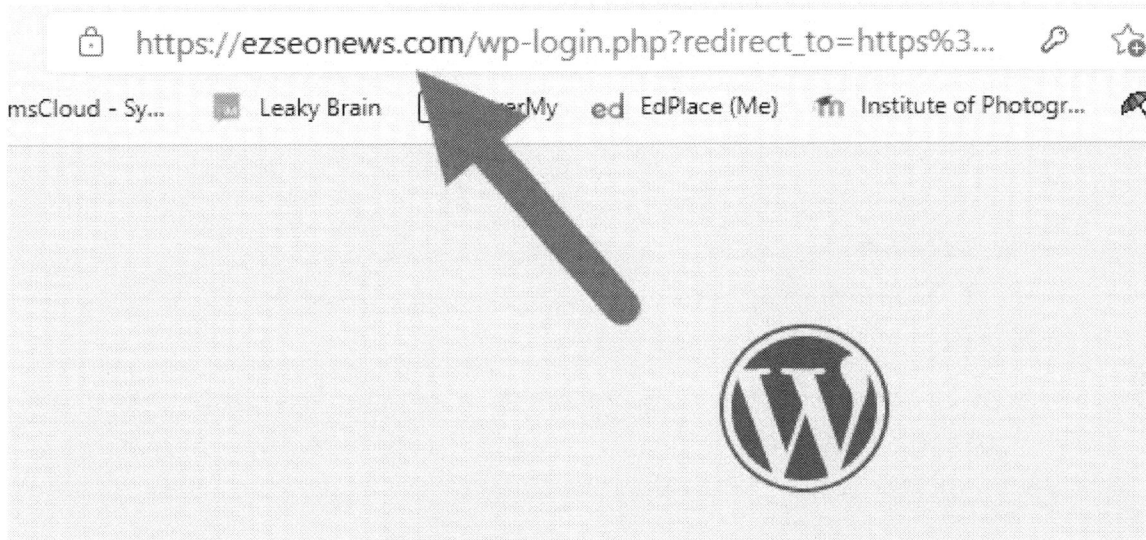

Here I am at one of my sites, and I can see the login form. However, get used to glancing up at the domain in the address bar before you log in. Make sure it's YOUR domain.

If a hacker can inject code into your website, they can set up a redirect. That means as you try to log in, you're taken to a completely different domain. This is one the hacker owns, and it'll have a dummy login form. You think you're logging into your site, but you're not. Then, as you enter your username and password, you've just given the hacker your login details.

Threat 4 – PHP Error Reporting

PHP is a widely used open-source programming language. It's great for most kinds of web development, so it's no surprise to learn that WordPress is coded in PHP.

Besides the WordPress core files, WordPress themes and plugins also add PHP code to your website. As with any kind of programming, bugs in the code can cause problems. WordPress will tell you when an error occurs, as well as the line of code that caused it. That's great for developers. Alas, hackers can also use these error messages to gain more information about your web server.

Fortunately, there's a way to stop WordPress from issuing these error reports, therefore disabling PHP error reporting.

The security plugin we install later in the book doesn't take care of this for you. If you want to disable error reporting, here's how you do it.

You need to add a special line of code to your wp-config.php file. You can find this file in the root folder of your domain.

The simple line of code is as follows: **error_reporting(0);**

Place the code right after the opening **<?php** tag and above all the other code in the file as per the image:

```
1  <?php
2
3  error_reporting(0);
4
5
6  /**
7    * The base configurations of the WordPr
8    *
9    * This file has the following configura
```

If you ever need to see the error messages in the future, simply come in and remove this line of code while you're working on your site. You can either delete it or comment it out using the format below:

/* error_reporting(0); */

The /* at the start and the */ at the end stop any commands inside from being read. When you've finished the work on your site, you can remove the comment markers to once again disable PHP error reporting.

Threat 5 - File Editor

The file editor inside your WordPress Dashboard is invaluable. It gives you — or any other admin user logged into your account — access to theme and plugin files.

To edit theme files, go to the **Appearance** menu and select **Theme Editor**.

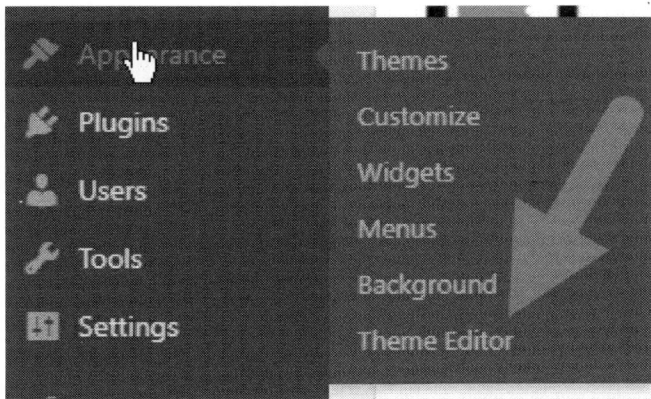

(To edit plugin files, go to the **Plugins** menu and select **Plugin Editor**).

The problem we have is that anyone with access to these files can "inject" malicious code into your website. So, if the logged-in user is a hacker, the consequences can be catastrophic.

The good news is you can disable these editors by adding a single line of code to your wp-config.php file.

I'm going to show you how to do this manually, but this is for information only. The plugin we install in the second part of this book will do the work for you.

For those who want to do this manually now, here's how it works.

This wp-config.php file is in the root folder of your website. You can gain access to it by using FTP or the File Manager inside cPanel.

Here's what it looks like when opened in a text editor:

I've drawn an arrow at the point where I'm going to insert the line of code.

Position your cursor in the blank line right before the line that starts:

// ** MySQL settings - ...

In this line, insert the following code:

define('DISALLOW_FILE_EDIT', true);

When you've done that, save your wp-config.php file and make sure it overwrites the older version.

Now log in to your WordPress Dashboard. You'll no longer see the options to use the editor. Here's how the Appearance menu looks now:

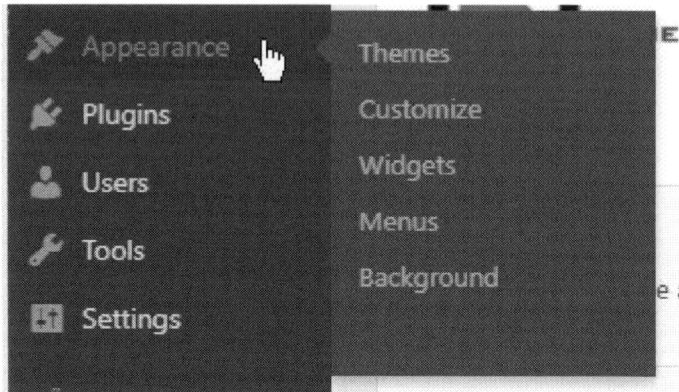

Here's the Plugins menu:

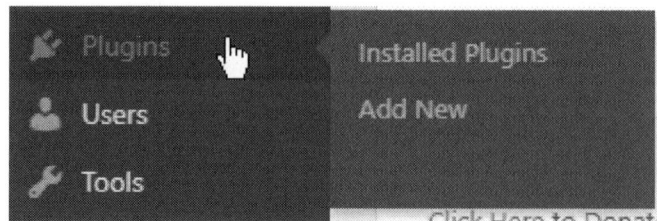

Threat 6 – Control the Content Published on Your Site

This is common sense, I know. It's still vital to realize how security issues can result from the stuff you publish.

When you create a page or post in WordPress, you have an option to embed code into that page or post. For example, it could be YouTube video code, JavaScript, or something else.

The only reason you add code to your pages is to add some form of functionality or feature. If you're non-technical, then you may not understand the code, and that's okay. But what is vitally important is that you trust the source. Remember, malicious code gives hackers a back door into your website or web server.

The "common sense" rules that apply here are:

1. Don't embed any code into a post or a page unless you trust the source 100% or know the code is safe.

For example, you know you can embed a YouTube video into your page, as Google owns YouTube. They are a trusted source.

If you're an affiliate marketer and you want to embed some affiliate code given to you by Amazon, then that is fine too. Amazon is another trusted source.

But if you join an unknown affiliate scheme and they ask you to embed code into your pages, get the code checked out. Only put it into your posts if you trust the person or company that gave it to you 100%.

2. Be careful if you allow other people to publish content on your site. I suggest you manually approve all new submissions before you publish them. The quick way to check the content is to switch over to the **Text** tab of the WordPress editor so you can see if there's any code in the article. Don't publish anything that contains code you were unaware of or are uncertain about.

3. If you allow visitors to leave comments, DON'T auto-approve them. Even comments can have code embedded into them. It's safer to check comments manually first and only approve them when you're sure.

IMPORTANT: There is an option in WordPress that allows you to auto-approve comments from visitors that have had at least one comment approved previously.

Before a comment appears	☐ Comment must be manually approved
	☑ Comment author must have a previously approved comment

Don't enable it.

This was the way a lot of WordPress sites got hacked in the past. A hacker would submit a good comment to get it approved manually. They'd then use their new "auto-approved" status to add comments with code embedded. It's much safer to moderate ALL comments manually.

Before a comment appears ➜ ☑ Comment must be manually approved
☐ Comment author must have a previously approved comment

We'll revisit comment security later in the book.

Threat 7 - New Users

A WordPress website can have more than one user.

A "user" in this context means anyone who can log in to the WordPress Dashboard. It has nothing to do with being a "visitor." A visitor is anyone who turns up to view your website in their web browser.

Some sites allow visitors to register as users, giving them login details to access the Dashboard. What they can do after they register depends on the privileges you give them. Privileges range from editing user profiles to complete control and administration of the site. You should give your users only the privileges they need, and no more.

At this point, you might wonder why a webmaster would allow visitors to become users. Here are some of the most popular reasons:

- To allow guest bloggers on the site. That is, allow your visitors to create posts (fresh content) on your site. This is usually in return for a link they include somewhere in the article. Unless you trust them and know exactly what you're doing, I don't recommend having guest bloggers post on your website. They pose a security problem, as well as an SEO headache.

- To create a membership site. If you decide you want to create a membership site, I recommend you use the **Wishlist Member** WordPress plugin. The plugin adds extra layers of security and gives you a lot more options for configuring and setting up your site. If you're interested in learning more, I have a course on building a membership site with **Wishlist Member**. There's a link to all my video courses at the end of this book.

- To create a mailing list of "subscribers." The best way to create a mailing list is to use proper third-party tools. One of the best ones for mailing lists and autoresponders is Aweber - http://ezseo.aweber.com. Companies like Aweber shield you from a lot of potential security (and hosting) issues. Security and hosting hassles can arise when you try to set this type of thing up on your domain.

For safety reasons, my advice is to NOT let unknown visitors register as users. There's a setting in the WordPress Dashboard you need to check.

Anyone can register

In the General Settings, make sure **Anyone can register** is unchecked like this:

Membership   ☐ Anyone can register

This should be off (unchecked) by default. It will only show as active if you, or someone else, checked it at some point.

If you choose to enable this option, I highly recommend you set the default role to "Subscriber." That'll give new users basic access without the opportunity to cause much damage. You can then change these roles as needed if you want to elevate a user's privileges at any point.

The options you have for roles are as follows:

- Subscriber: can manage their profile.
- Contributor: can write guest posts but not publish them (best option).
- Author: can write and publish their posts.
- Editor: Can write, publish and manage ALL posts.
- Administrator: full access to the site and all administrative screens.
- Super Admin: a network administrator when using networked WordPress (not an option with the regular version of WordPress).

If you decide to allow visitors to register as users, only give them the privileges they need and no more. This is the most important piece of advice I can give you, so please take heed.

Usernames & Passwords

We looked at usernames and passwords earlier in the book and how important they are to keep your site safe. The same is true for ALL users on your site. If you have multiple users, your site is only as secure as its weakest link.

When you allow other users to register, you need to make sure they all use very secure usernames and passwords.

Although WordPress automatically generates a secure password for each new user, they can still edit their profile. That means they can also change their password. Don't ever let users change their secure password for an insecure one.

Threat 8 - Widgets & Code

Earlier in the book, we looked at why you need to control the content of your site and the common-sense rules surrounding published content. We saw code as one potential problem. I want to revisit code here because widgets can pose a threat.

For example, the Custom HTML and text widgets can contain any text you like, including code. Here is a Custom HTML widget on one of my websites:

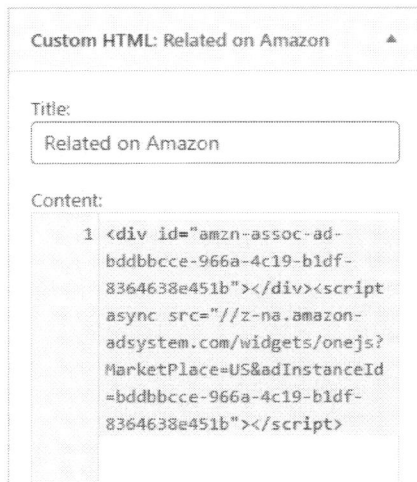

```
Custom HTML: Related on Amazon          ▲

Title:
Related on Amazon

Content:
1  <div id="amzn-assoc-ad-
   bddbbcce-966a-4c19-b1df-
   8364638e451b"></div><script
   async src="//z-na.amazon-
   adsystem.com/widgets/onejs?
   MarketPlace=US&adInstanceId
   =bddbbcce-966a-4c19-b1df-
   8364638e451b"></script>
```

The code above is a script and displays some recommended products in the sidebar. I understand the code and know it's safe to use, so it's fine. But what if you don't understand what the code does or what it means?

Let's recap the common-sense rules again:

- Only put code into your posts, pages and widgets if you trust the source and know the code is trustworthy.

- Only install widgets (installed as plugins) if you trust the source of the plugin 100%.

- Plugins and themes you get from the official WordPress repositories should be safe. For your part, you still need to update them regularly in case any vulnerability issues need fixing. Keeping themes and plugins up to date minimizes the risk from hackers.

- If you buy themes or plugins from other websites, is the source trustworthy? Do your due diligence on Google and read any reviews. Are there customer comments that concern you?

Embedding Code in a Post or Page

I want to show you a bit of code to highlight a potential issue. You will see how easy it is to spot once you know what to look for.

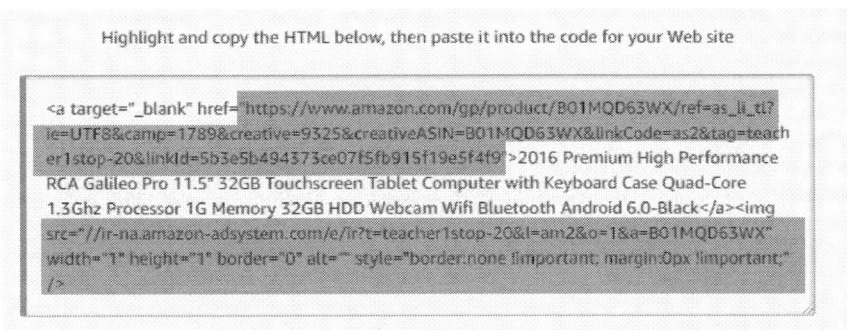

```
Highlight and copy the HTML below, then paste it into the code for your Web site

<a target="_blank" href="https://www.amazon.com/gp/product/B01MQD63WX/ref=as_li_tl?
ie=UTF8&camp=1789&creative=9325&creativeASIN=B01MQD63WX&linkCode=as2&tag=teach
er1stop-20&linkId=5b3e5b494373ce07f5fb915f19e5f4f9">2016 Premium High Performance
RCA Galileo Pro 11.5" 32GB Touchscreen Tablet Computer with Keyboard Case Quad-Core
1.3Ghz Processor 1G Memory 32GB HDD Webcam Wifi Bluetooth Android 6.0-Black</a><img
src="//ir-na.amazon-adsystem.com/e/ir?t=teacher1stop-20&l=am2&o=1&a=B01MQD63WX"
width="1" height="1" border="0" alt="" style="border:none !important; margin:0px !important;"
/>
```

This code is from Amazon and is safe.

What I want you to look out for are URLs that don't belong to your site. The code above has two. If you know any HTML, you'll know that the first mention of Amazon.com is the URL for a text link. The second is an image displayed with the advert. This is all fine because we understand the code.

But what if you get some code you don't understand.

Take this example:

Copy Ad Code

```
<script type="text/javascript">amazon_ad_tag ="santschri-21"; amazon_ad_width ="120";
amazon_ad_height ="600"; </script><script src="http://ir-uk.amazon-adsystem.com/s/ads.js">
</script>
```

OK, the URL is to amazon-adsystem.com. I assume it's an Amazon-controlled domain, so it is safe. If you're unsure, you can check with a quick search on Google. Just search Google for the domain and see what comes back. In this case, it's a legitimate domain used by Amazon to serve ads. You need to verify any suspicious or unfamiliar URLs found in the code you add to your posts or pages.

IMPORTANT: That URL calls some JavaScript (JS) code (ads.js). You don't get to see the actual JS code that'll be running on your site. It could be anything and do pretty much what it wants on your page(s). Can you see why you need to trust the code you add 100%?

Threat 9 - Plugins

Plugins are pieces of code that add new features to your WordPress site.

Since code can control pretty much every aspect of a site, including malicious things, you need to be sure you can trust the plugins you use.

Although much of this is also common sense, here are a few helpful tips:

- Only install plugins from trusted sources. The WordPress repository is the main trusted source. But what if you find a plugin on a website that isn't in the repository. In this case, do your due diligence and check out reviews and customer comments on those plugins.

- Developers who create free plugins come in two forms. There are the good guys who are happy to help and want to create a useful, free plugin with no strings attached. Then there are those who want to profit from their free plugin. There are several ways to do this. The most common method is to give away a free trial version. They hope you'll upgrade to a paid version with more features and functions after the trial period. These can be fine but again, do your due diligence.

  The type of plugin to be wary of are those which include code that doesn't directly contribute to the functionality you're trying to gain. For example, a mortgage calculator that adds a link back to the lender's website. In this case, you want the functionality of the calculator. Yet, the bank has included other, unrelated code to that function. In this case, it's a link pointing back to their website. My advice is to avoid this type of plugin at all costs.

- Always keep plugins up to date. Be wary of those that have no known updates or have not had an update in a very long time. There are also legitimate plugins that just don't get updates. For example, they use secure code, and the author doesn't want to add new features. These are fine. If there's a plugin you want, but it's been a while since its last update, check it out on Google. Use a search term like "plugin name + security" to see if there are any reported issues.

- If you deactivate a plugin, uninstall it altogether. Even inactive plugins CAN cause security problems if they contain vulnerable code.

Threat 10 - Themes

Themes, like plugins, add code to your website.

The same kind of common-sense measures we talked about for plugins also apply to themes. Here are some guidelines.

- The WordPress theme repository is a safe place to get themes. Many people still want to look further afield to find the best themes for their website. Be careful where you get yours from. Again, do a search on Google for the theme in question and see whether it appears to be from a trusted source.

- Some authors offer free themes. They usually include a link in the footer (or elsewhere) back to the developer's website. On the face of it, the deal looks sweet. NEVER use a theme that forces this type of site-wide link on you, no matter how subtle. Why? You have no control over the destination website attached to that link. The link may redirect, either now or later on, to any site the author chooses, e.g., porn, gambling, and so on. This type of site-wide footer link will also cause you SEO problems in Google. The search engines don't like them, not even if the site it links to is a trusted one.

- Keep themes up to date and install updates as soon as you know about them. Theme developers might release an update to add new features, but it could also be to plug security holes.

Threat 11 - Comment Spam

Comments are an important part of any WordPress website. They allow visitors to leave valuable feedback about the site's content. It's a great way to engage in a conversation with you, the webmaster, and other visitors on your website. Google likes sites that have this type of interaction. Therefore, it makes good sense to have comments enabled. There is a "but" though. Comments can also pose a real threat to your website security.

In the past, hackers have used comments to gain access to websites. They did this using something called the Zero-Day Exploit. The exploit involved hackers inserting malicious JavaScript into a simple comment. Once you approved their comment from the WordPress Dashboard, the door opened. The hacker got remote access to the site, control passwords, and add administrative users, etc. In other words, they had total control over the affected website.

If you want to research it more, this type of exploit is a good example of a "cross-scripting attack."

For the exploit to work, the webmaster had to approve the hacker's comment. That was the first hurdle for them. Fortunately for the hackers, some sites are set up to auto-approve comments IF the person had a previous comment approved.

The hacker would begin their hack by leaving a great comment, knowing the webmaster would most likely approve it. Once accepted, they'd follow it up with a malicious comment, realizing that some sites would auto-approve it.

Look at this setting in the discussion panel:

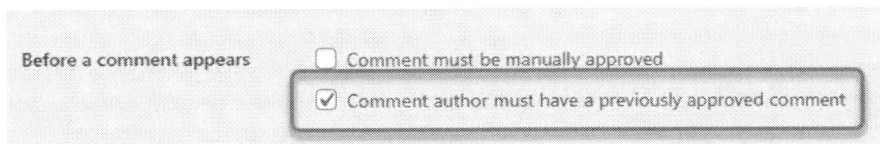

Before a comment appears
☐ Comment must be manually approved
☑ Comment author must have a previously approved comment

As things stand, if a commenter has a previously approved comment, any new ones would be auto-approved. WordPress versions between 3.9 and 4.2 were vulnerable to this hack. The developers have since patched more current versions to prevent these attacks from happening.

So now your site is up to date and safe against the Zero-Day exploit. But hackers are smart people, and they're always looking for new ways. For that reason, I recommend you always check the first box in that section.

Comments must be manually approved.

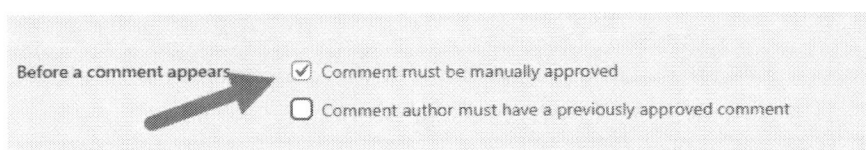

Before a comment appears
☑ Comment must be manually approved
☐ Comment author must have a previously approved comment

Now you have to manually approve ALL comments. This way, you can check the comment for code before you accept it. Moderating comments is also a good way to make sure no nasty language or hostilities end up on your pages.

Links in Comments

When a visitor leaves a comment, they have two opportunities to insert links into it. They can add a URL in the URL box of the comment section, or they can insert a link into the body of the actual comment:

Leave a Comment

Your email address will not be published. Required fields are marked *

Type here.

Name* Email* Website

Post Comment »

Here is a nice simple rule to follow for comments:

Always **nofollow** links in the comments section of your site. The "nofollow" attribute tells search engines not to let the link influence a site's rankings. In other words, ignore it, don't follow it. You do this because you have no control over where these links point. Whoever controls the URL in the link can point it wherever they like, but you're not responsible for it.

Fortunately, the WordPress default is to nofollow links in comments. However, some plugins allow you to make them dofollow. The advantage is that dofollow sites encourage more comments. People like them because dofollow links are valuable for off-page SEO purposes. My advice is to avoid the temptation and don't do it. If someone only leaves a comment because they want the backlink, it's likely to be a poor comment to have anyway.

Here are some other comment tips:

- Manually approve ALL comments.
- Only approve comments that genuinely add value to your page, i.e., they contribute to the conversation.
- Use a spam filter like Akismet to filter spam comments.

- Don't approve a comment if the author of the comment has filled the name field with keywords.

- Don't approve comments with links in the body of the comment unless those links point to high-authority sites you trust. If the comment is good but has unwanted links, you can always strip out the links and then approve it.

- Never approve a comment that is trying to flatter your ego. Comments like "great post" or "cool information" are pure spam. Treat them as such.

Most comment spam tips are good common sense, but it never hurts to recap.

Threat 12 – Limit Login Attempts

When a hacker tries to get into a site, they might use special software tools. They use these to launch something called a brute force attack.

Their software programs try thousands, or hundreds of thousands, of usernames and password combinations. They can do this in a very short space of time. The way to prevent attacks of this type is to limit the number of login attempts.

If a user fails to log in after X attempts, the system locks their IP address for a set length of time. Once the time expires, they can try to log in again. It's a sensible precaution. It's there so that genuine users — who accidentally mistype their passwords — can access their site after the lockout period. As for the hackers, the delay is usually long enough for them to give up and move on to an easier target.

The plugin we install and set up in the second part of the book will limit login attempts for us. There's no need for you to do anything about it just yet.

Threat 13 – 2-Factor Authentication

You may already have this set up for your Gmail account or another online system. It adds a great level of security to your website by requiring TWO forms of authentication.

For example, first, you go to a login form and enter your username and password (the first form of authentication). They then send a special code to your mobile phone. You then enter the code into a form (second authentication) in the login process. You can only log in to your site after successfully entering the code.

It's more hassle, but it does add an extra level of security to your site, and that's always a good thing.

The plugin we install later does not offer 2-factor authentication. If you want to add this to your site, you have other options. I recommend you search the WordPress plugin repository for "Google Authenticator."

You'll find a lot of plugins that offer this functionality. Look for one with good reviews and with recent updates. Here's a good example:

Google Authenticator – WordPress Two Factor Authentication (2FA , MFA)

Install Now

More Details

Google Authenticator, Two Factor Authentication (2 Factor), OTP verificaion - SMS and Email, Apps like Microsoft, Duo, LastPass & more on login an ...

By miniOrange

★★★★⯪ (285)

20,000+ Active Installations   ✔ Compatible with your version of WordPress

This plugin is free for one user. If you want to protect more than one site, you'll need to sign up for one of their plans or find a different plugin.

After you install and activate it, you'll see a new menu item in the sidebar labeled miniOrange 2-Factor. When you click on that, it takes you to a simple setup screen.

I won't go into detail on how to set this up, but it's fairly intuitive. On the Setup Two-Factor tab, you can select the method of the verification, including:

- Email
- SMS
- Phone Call verification

Is this type of protection worth setting up? Well, that's up to you. I find it a little too much hassle, so I don't use it on my websites.

Threat 14 – Login Page Protection

The login page for your website is the main gateway to access your Dashboard. It's often the first port of call for hackers.

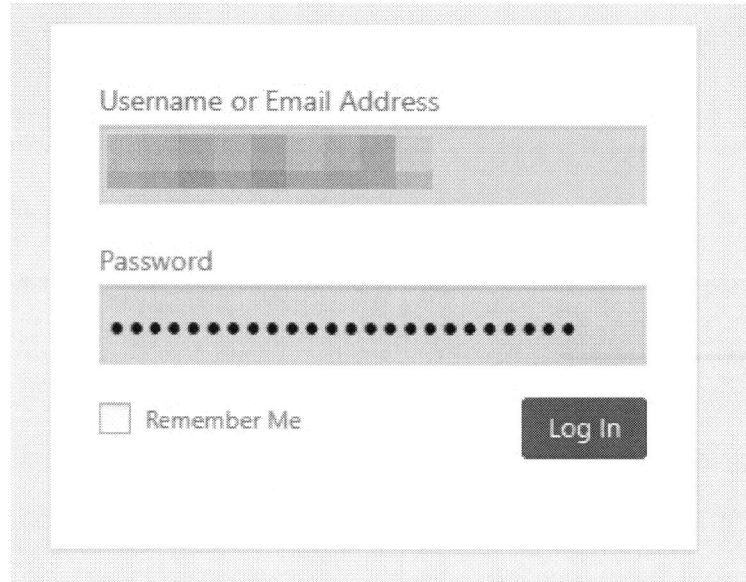

If you protect your login page, you reduce the chance of a hacker gaining access.

Fortunately, there are a few ways to protect the login page. You can rename it, move it, add a Captcha, or block certain IP addresses.

Some methods of protection are more effective than others. The plugin we install in the last part of this book gives us some great options, so no need to worry about this right now.

Threat 15 - Database Table Prefix

Earlier in the book, we looked at backing up your WordPress websites. You saw how this was the only way to protect your site 100% from any major issues. If you remember, there were two elements to back up, namely:

1. Site files
2. Site database

WordPress uses a MySQL database that contains several "tables." Tables are simply spreadsheets of data. WordPress uses a number of these tables to store related information.

For example, the "users" table contains data about the users, like username and password, email address, and so on.

The "posts" table will have all the posts you've ever created. It will include the date, excerpt, post name, title, and content, etc.

Each table in the database has a name, and WordPress creates these names at the install stage. You do have some control over the name of each table as these names have a prefix. WordPress, by default, used the prefix: wp_

In the case of the "users table," the name will be wp_users.

The security problem arises when the webmaster uses this default prefix. If a hacker knows your prefix, they know the name of every table in your database. Because of this, you must change your default prefix.

You're in luck if you use Softaculous to install WordPress on your server. It randomly generates a prefix for your install. That means no more wp_ default.

Don't worry if you have an existing site that still uses the wp_ prefix. The plugin we install and setup later in the book gives you an easy way to change it.

Threat 16 – WordPress Security Keys & Salts

WordPress developers introduced security keys in version 2.6, and they've been with us ever since. They initially added them to encrypt the cookie information stored on the visitor's computer.

As WordPress evolved, they added more and more of these security keys. You can find them in the wp-config.php file. Automated WordPress installer software generates these for you during the install process.

You need these keys because they add an extra layer of security to your site. They encrypt vital information like passwords.

```
/**#@+
 * Authentication Unique Keys and Salts.
 *
 * Change these to different unique phra
 * You can generate these using the {@li    https://api.wordpress.org/secret-key/1.1/salt/    ordPress.org secret-key service}
 * You can change these at any point in                                               force all users to have to log in
 *
 * @since 2.6.0
 */
define( 'AUTH_KEY',         'gf+E|y.^xVvNb^pYw$xY~T<vTJUoR2+{r<szg9~R$II9xg:E:(=3@3]awEm^e[9I' );
define( 'SECURE_AUTH_KEY',  '2WAWm!8K(-a:(pc@zC3cSG*4,Bqh??}RSi!X(SA][TxM@nnF*kEw~08I5o|M1O=m' );
define( 'LOGGED_IN_KEY',    '4$F =(pQMUxr3!XBS(`2kC5yshXf0m9s/Fwu9f<F    t5?!~ArWs(h4Qjgzm1CsQ' );
define( 'NONCE_KEY',        'PXhG0G{ p[^P(MhYj!Use|0%.CNvXLt.D0          nbw!dT6+@`nwk)`3X*d0' );
define( 'AUTH_SALT',        ']bZ*|s]<rpo|YJe|>AMoOUF%;D|2GEu$[x
define( 'SECURE_AUTH_SALT', ';O9@7~`_25M*_6VcCu_7S]Xo4gTk$qJT3TGpS         s?lqJ<CO(+,
define( 'LOGGED_IN_SALT',   'vrYEb1^A$(KPAD7>_eh77hf|9KuP_hcofPYAMuA^j(d`-1Rr]?r-0#M/i,y+2TgG' );
define( 'NONCE_SALT',       ';krE-*EJx$NUsGT]L&tY1VQp;e*<!&nH_>FY(AtsvN>,6.,<0X<~K-6_P9zeIr_K' );

/**#@-*/
```

If you install WordPress manually, you'll need to generate them yourself and copy them into the wp-config.php file. There's a URL included in the wp-config-sample.php file that generates your unique keys & salts.

A WordPress salt is simply a random string of data. What it does is hashes (transforms) the WordPress security keys in the wp-config.php file. These security keys & salts are long. Fortunately, you don't need to remember them.

There's good news if you already have WordPress installed. These keys are more than likely already generated and residing in your wp-config.php file. If they're not, you can add them manually, though this won't be necessary with automated installers. The only time you need to add them by hand is if you manually install WordPress. Few people have reasons to take the manual route these days.

Threat 17 - XML-RPC

XML-RPC is a programming interface (API). What it does is allow programmers and developers to talk to WordPress.

A lot of tools may need XML-RPC to work properly. For example, I use Open Live Writer to work offline on my websites. This gives me a WYSIWYG (What You See Is What You Get) editor. I use it to create and format posts or pages that I can then publish to my site when I'm ready. Open Live Writer requires XML-RPC to be enabled for it to work.

Some plugins also need XML-RPC, like Jetpack.

Since WordPress 3.5, XML-RPC is enabled by default.

The problem we have is that software can manipulate WordPress through the XML-RPC. This makes it a possible security concern. A lot of WordPress gurus recommend you disable it.

In the past, hackers used XML-RPC for something called DDoS attacks. It stands for "Denial of Service."

Plugins like Akismet can usually spot this type of attack and prevent it. Therefore, it may not be worth switching off XML-RPC to stop DDoS attacks.

Hackers also extensively used XML-RPC for brute force attacks. But again, most security plugins will prevent this type of attack today, so it's not worth worrying about. The plugin we setup later also prevents this type of attack.

My suggestion is not to disable it. If you decide you want to, then some plugins can disable it for you. Check out this one:

STOP XML-RPC

Disable XML-RPC-API

A simple and lightweight plugin to disable XML-RPC API, X-Pingback and pingback-ping in WordPress 3.5+...

By Neatmarketing

Install Now

More Details

★★★★★ (11)

5,000+ Active Installations

Last Updated: 3 weeks ago

✔ Compatible with your version of WordPress

Threat 18 – Web Hosting

The threat most people don't even think about is the hosting company they use for their website. You need to do a few checks and be aware that the cheapest option is not always the best.

If a web host offers cheap hosting, it can mean the following:

- Plenty of people who want cheap hosting will be signing up.

- Accepts any type of site, meaning your website may be on the same server as porn, gambling, and other undesirable topics. These may be more vulnerable to hacking attempts because of their content.

- They will likely cut a few corners. Security costs money, so it could be one of the weaker aspects of your host.

At the very least, you should:

- Check what version of PHP and MySQL (or MariaDB) the web host uses. These are both required for WordPress sites and should be kept up to date. This minimizes the chance of any security breaches.

- Ask your host what other security measures they take to protect your website. Do they regularly back their servers up? And in the event of a disaster, would they reinstate your site for free or a fee? How often do they carry out server maintenance? Anything specific to prevent hackers?

Threat 19 - wp-config.php

The wp-config.php file contains sensitive information. This includes things like security keys & salts, usernames, passwords, and database names, etc.

If a hacker gets hold of this file, they'd be a lot closer to hacking into your site. For this reason alone, it's a good idea to protect the file in any way you can.

One way to do this is to move the file to a folder above your WordPress installation directory. Some people will tell you this is a good idea, while other security experts will disagree. I don't do this.

An alternative is to put the following code into the .htaccess file for your website.

<files wp-config.php>
order allow, deny
deny from all
</files>

Like this:

```
<files wp-config.php>
order allow, deny
deny from all
</files>

# BEGIN WordPress
<IfModule mod_rewrite.c>
RewriteEngine On
RewriteBase /
RewriteRule ^index\.php$ - [L]
RewriteCond %{REQUEST_FILENAME} !-f
RewriteCond %{REQUEST_FILENAME} !-d
RewriteRule . /index.php [L]
</IfModule>

# END WordPress
```

Mac computers hide the .htaccess file by default, so you'll need to "unhide" all files to find it on your server.

Adding the above code will stop anyone from accessing this file. If you need to open it, you can do that via your cPanel's File Manager or FTP.

So should you add this code to your .htaccess file?

I don't, but that's my personal choice. I don't add it because the plugin we install later adds so many other good layers of protection. Because of this, I think both the above methods are unnecessary.

Threat 20 – File Permissions

Files on a web server, just like files on a computer, have certain permissions. These permissions define who or what can access, read and/or write to those files.

Your files need tight controls. We don't want a hacker to come along and be able to access them, or worst still, change them around.

The permissions you see on a web host are a little different from what you see on a PC. Your typical PC files will have something like read-only or writable. On a web server, you'll see the permissions as numbers.

I took the following screenshot from an FTP program. Here it shows the file permissions on one of my WordPress files:

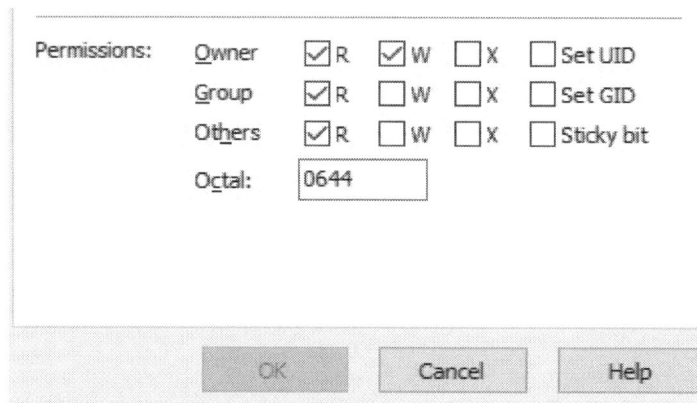

You can see that three groups have permissions:

1. Owner
2. Group
3. Others

The possible permissions for each of these groups of users are:

- R – Read
- W -Write
- X – Execute (or run the file).

Note that the permission for this file is 0644 (in the 'Octal' box). So 644 is a number made up from the permissions table above. Each of these permissions has a value.

Example: For owners, the Read permission has a value of 400 and a Write value of 200. Execute would add 100 points to this permissions value.

For "Group," the Read permission has a value of 40 and a Write a value of 20. You may be able to guess the execute permission for the group has a value of 10.

For "Others," Read, Write and Execute are an order of 10 smaller, so 4, 2, and 1 respectively.

In the screenshot above, you can do simple maths. We have:

- Owner read (400) and write (200) = 600 total.
- Groups read (40) = 40 total.
- Others read (4) = 4 total.

Therefore, the total permission for this file is 600+40+4 = 644

Fortunately, you don't need to remember any of this. I'll give you a guide to what permissions your files and folders should have, and you can check them if you want. The security plugin we install later checks and fixes permission issues for you anyway. There's nothing for you to do at the moment.

Expected File Permissions

- All directories should be 755.
- All files should be 644, including the wp-config.php, .htaccess, and wp-admin/index.php files.

OK, on that note, we've now finished this section of the book. You now know the majority of security issues that relate to WordPress and how to fix them. In the second part of the book, we install and set up a single security plugin. This will protect your WordPress site against most threats discussed so far.

SECTION 2 – Secure Your Website with a Plugin

The first part of this book was an introduction to the types of protection you should use on your website. Some of these measures are a little technical to put into place. Fortunately, there's a great WordPress plugin that'll add most of these layers. Best of all is that it uses a simple point-and-click interface. In this section of the book, we install our smart security plugin and configure it for your site.

Chapter 5 – Installing the Plugin

The plugin I recommend is called the "All In One WP Security & Firewall" plugin. You can find it by clicking the 'Add New' link in the Plugins menu and searching for it. This is what it looks like:

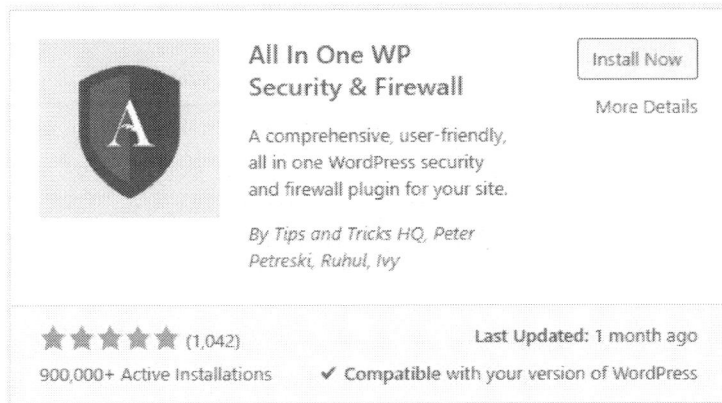

Install and activate it now.

You'll see a "WP Security" menu item in the Dashboard. If you move your mouse over WP Security, the popup menu looks like this:

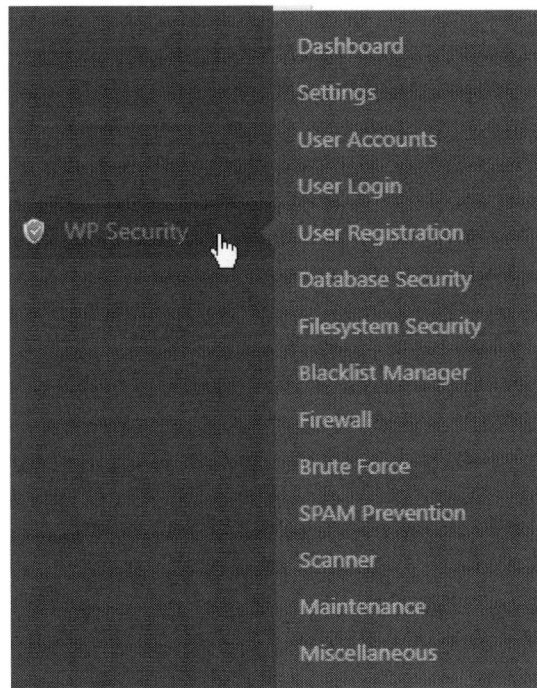

Each item in the popup menu opens a page of settings you can change.

Click on the "Dashboard" link in the menu. You'll get a graphical interpretation of the current security measures on your site.

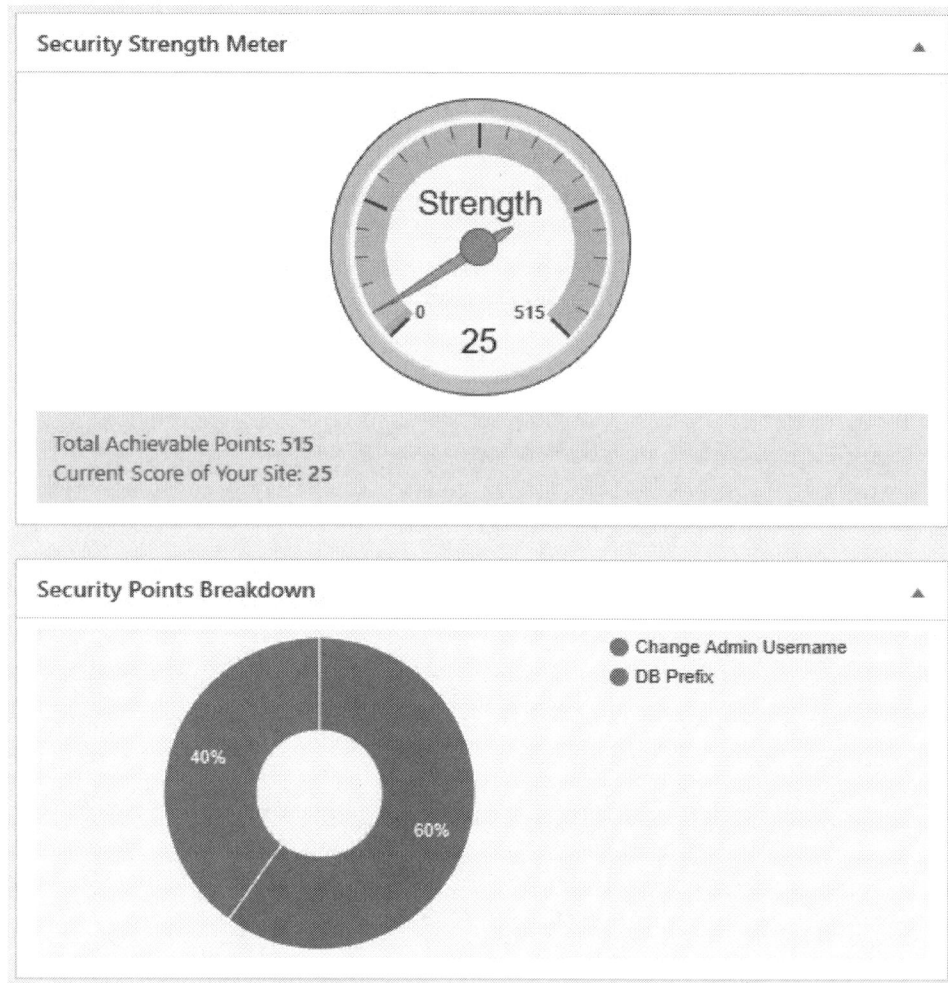

The **Security Strength Meter** gives you an indication of how secure your site is right now. It is a points-based scoring system, so the more points you have, the more security measures you have in place. Currently, my site scores just 25 out of a total of 515 points available.

The **Security Points Breakdown** will list some of the security measures that are already in place. On my site, I don't have "admin" as my username, and my database prefix is not the old default "wp_." These two measures make it more difficult for hackers, but as the 25 out of 515 points suggest, there is still a lot to do.

Both of these graphics will look a lot different by the time we're finished.

Before we start to make any changes to the site's security, there's one very important task you need to do.

Chapter 6 – Backup Important Files

This plugin makes changes to some of the WordPress files on your server. These changes are necessary to keep hackers out. In rare cases, though, they could break your site or make it difficult for you to log in to the Dashboard.

Don't panic. It's quite uncommon for this to happen. Even so, we're going to make backups of important files before we start. This is just a precaution in case anything goes wrong. In the event of any problems, you can simply use the backups to restore the file that causes issues.

The good news is that once you find a configuration that works for you, you won't have any problems down the line. In other words, the only time you may encounter issues is when you initially set up the plugin. We're going to go through things in some detail, and I'll inform you of any potential problems along the way. I'll also show you how to recover your site if a setting in the plugin breaks something.

You can back up all the important files from within the plugin itself. From the WP Security menu, select **Settings**.

In the WP Security Plugin section on the **General Settings** tab, you'll see what needs backing up:

The three essential items to back up are:

- Database
- .htaccess file
- wp-config.php file

With backups of these three things, we can recover from any problem we may encounter during the plugin setup stages. You'll notice that these three items are links. These links take you to the tool that can back up that item.

Backup the Database

Click the link to **Back up your database** link. This will open a new tab in your browser and take you to the DB Backup tab within the plugin settings.

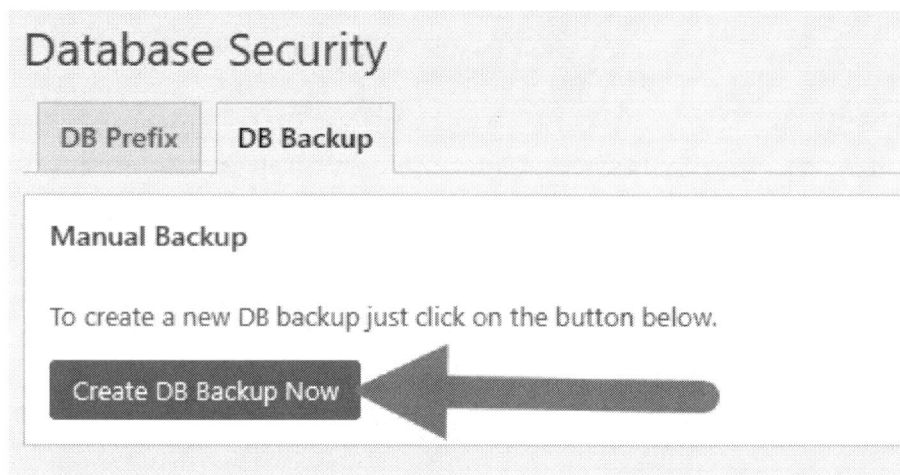

Click the button to '**Create a DB Backup Now.**'

Once the backup is complete, you'll get a message on the screen to show you where the backed up file is on your server:

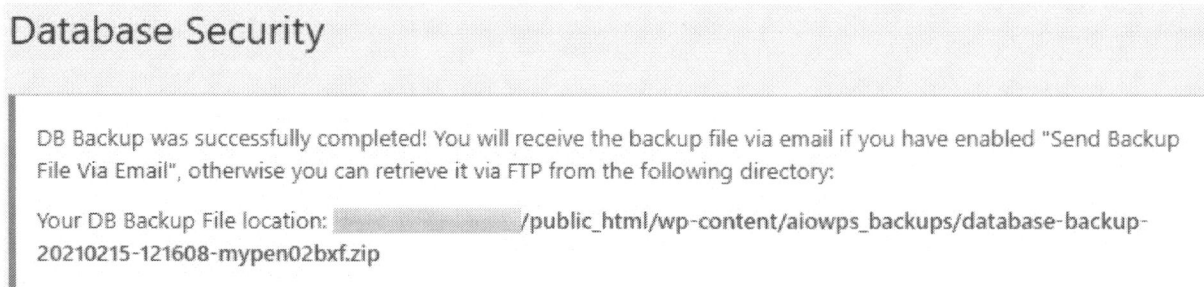

I suggest you login to your webspace — via FTP or File Manager in cPanel — and download the backup to your computer.

Once done, go back to the general settings tab of the plugin and click the second link to **Backup .htaccess file**. Again, this will open a new tab in your browser. You'll see the **Backup .htaccess File** button, so click on that. You'll get a message to confirm a successful backup and its location. Download the file to the same folder on your computer as the database backup.

Finally, click the **Backup wp-config.php file** button to open a new tab with an option to back up this file. In this case, the file downloads automatically to your computer. I suggest you then copy it to the same folder as your database and .htaccess files.

Now you have the three important files safely on your computer in case of a problem.

In the next chapter, we look at the steps to take if the plugin locks you out of your website.

Chapter 7 – If You Get Locked Out

Locked out of your WordPress Dashboard? Don't worry! You can quickly return your website to its previous state. We can do this by restoring one or two files. I'll show you how to do that now.

You can work with the files on your server in a couple of ways:

- FTP (File Transfer Protocol, using an FTP Client software tool).
- File Manager in cPanel.

I like to use FTP. It's faster and more convenient than going through the cumbersome File Manager inside cPanel. If you don't know how to set FTP up for your web server, ask your web host. Alternatively, you can always use the File Manager inside cPanel to make the necessary changes.

IP Lockout

One of the main reasons the plugin locks people out is if their IP address triggers the security settings. If it locks your IP address, you won't be able to login to your Dashboard with that particular IP.

The simplest solution is to use a VPN. This lets you change the IP on your computer as if you were in a different location, even a different country. There are a lot available; just search Google for VPN service.

When the system logged me out in the past, the first thing I would do is change my IP using a VPN service. I'd then log in and make the necessary changes to the plugin settings. I'd say this works fine in 99% of all cases, without the need to restore any files.

If you don't have, or want to buy a VPN service, then work your way through the next section.

Disabling the All In One Security Plugin

The quickest way to fix the issue is to disable the All In One Security plugin and reverse any changes it made. This is a 2-step process.

Step 1. Disable the plugin

Step 2. Reverse any changes the plugin made.

Step 1. Disable the Plugin

If you cannot log into your dashboard, you may be wondering how you can disable the plugin. The answer is to log into your hosting account and use the File Manager tool there. For cPanel hosting, log into cPanel and open up File Manager.

Navigate to the folder where WordPress is installed. You'll be able to tell you are there because you'll see the following folders:

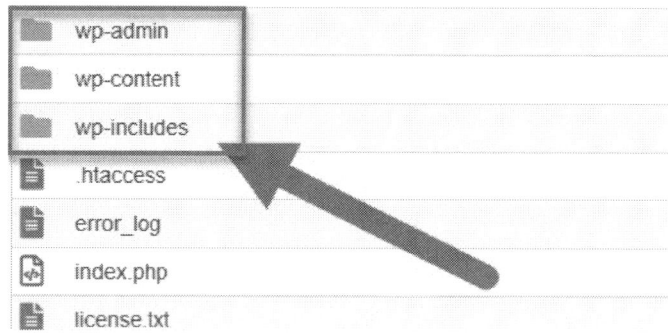

Open the wp-content folder and then the plugins folder inside that:

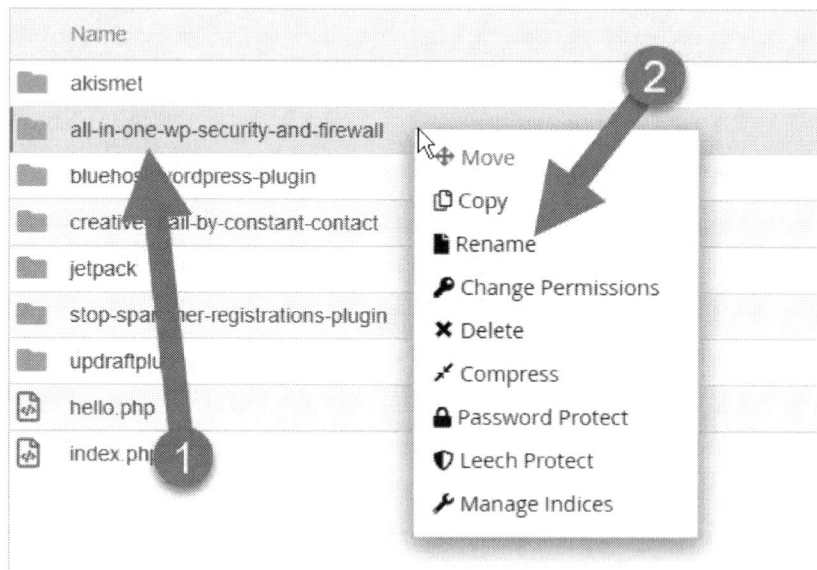

You'll see a folder for each plugin installed in WordPress. Right-click the one for the All In One Security plugin and click **Rename**.

Add **-old** to the end of the filename (you can add anything you like):

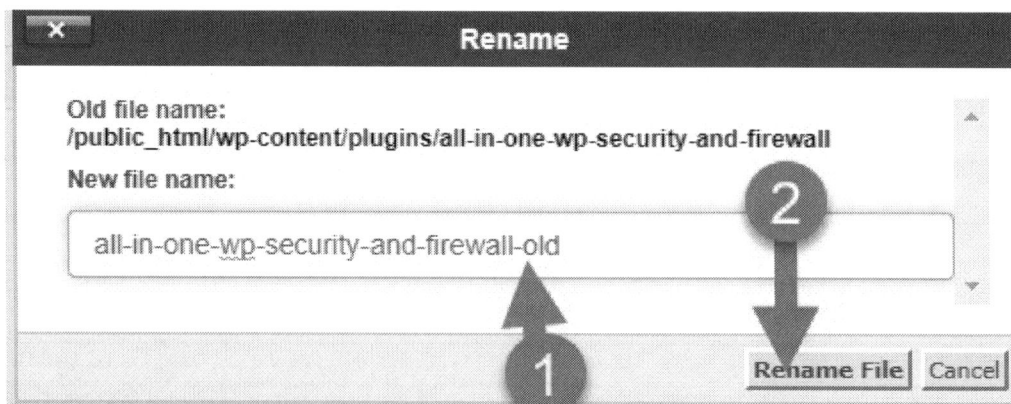

Now click the rename button.

With step 1 complete, you should be able to log into the dashboard.

Step 2 - Reverse Changes made by the plugin

The All In One Security plugin made some changes that uninstalling does not reverse. For that, you need a free plugin from this site:

https://www.tipsandtricks-hq.com/all-in-one-wp-security-reset-settings-plugin

(If you search Google for the **All In One Security reset plugin**, you will find it).

Download and install the plugin following the instructions on that web page if needed.

Once activated, go to the **Settings, AOIWPS Reset**:

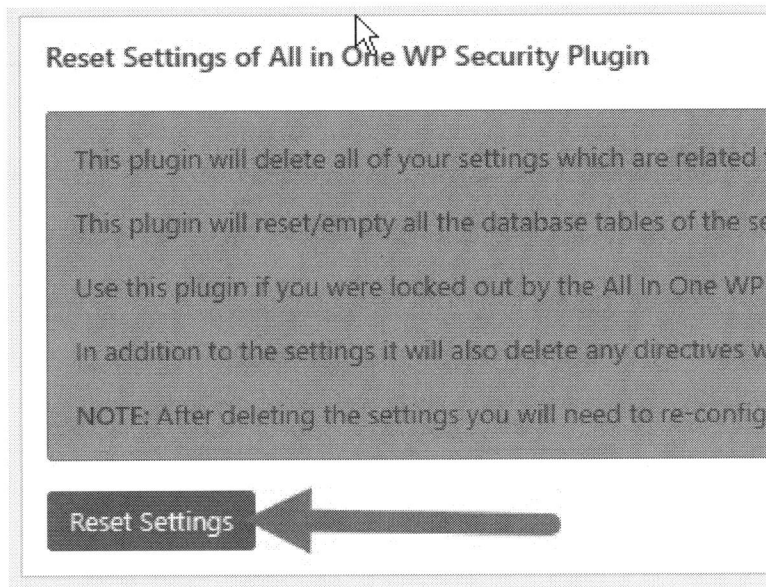

Reset Settings of All in One WP Security Plugin

This plugin will delete all of your settings which are related t

This plugin will reset/empty all the database tables of the se

Use this plugin if you were locked out by the All In One WP

In addition to the settings it will also delete any directives wi

NOTE: After deleting the settings you will need to re-config

Reset Settings

Click the **Reset Settings** button.

You can now uninstall this plugin. Also, log out of your dashboard.

Back in the File Manager of your cPanel, rename the plugin folder by removing the **-old** suffix in the same way you added it.

Now log back into your Dashboard and go to the **Plugins** screen.

You'll see the All In One Security plugin is there and deactivated. You can now activate it again.

The settings for the plugin that locked you out will have been reset, so be careful going forward. Don't enable something that locked you out previously.

The Last Option in case all else fails is: Restoring Files

If the previous option fails, and it never has for me, there is one final option. Restoring files from backup.

The problem with restoring files is that you lose all customizations to the plugin settings since the last backup. In other words, say you took the backup before you began to configure the plugin. This means — after the restoration — you'll have to reconfigure it all again from the start.

One thing that can make life a little easier is if you back up the files periodically as you set up the plugin. Then, if a problem does arise, you can restore the files starting with the most recent backup. If necessary, you can work backward until you find the backup file that fixes the issue.

So, you need your backup files to restore your site in the event of a problem. We saved those to your computer in the last chapter.

The chance is you'll only need to restore the .htaccess file as it's where the plugin makes most of its changes. If WordPress does lock you out, I recommend you try to restore functionality in the following order:

1. Restore the .htaccess file and check to see if you can get in. If you can, you don't need to follow step 2. If you can't, keep reading.

2. Restore the wp-config.php file and check to see if you can get in.

After completing steps one and two, you should have access to your site. If not, then clear cookies in your browser and try again.

If you still can't get in, I recommend you go and rename your "plugins" folder. This is the last resort, but it does work. You can then log in, but you'll get some error messages. Ignore them. While you're logged in, rename the plugins folder back to its correct name and refresh the browser. You should now be able to access the Security settings and make the changes.

I've never seen an instance where you'd need to restore the database because of the security plugin. The database backup is very useful in case your site gets hacked, and you need to restore the content. However, for a full backup, I recommend you look at the Updraft plugin we mentioned earlier.

Restoring the .htaccess file

This is simply a matter of uploading your backup and overwriting the existing .htaccess file in the root folder of your site.

First, it's worth having a look at the .htaccess file on your server. You'll see it contains some comments that pinpoint the changes made by the plugin:

```
# BEGIN All In One WP Security
#AIOWPS_BASIC_HTACCESS_RULES_START
<Files .htaccess>
<IfModule mod_authz_core.c>
Require all denied
</IfModule>
<IfModule !mod_authz_core.c>
Order deny,allow
Deny from all
```

Comments start with the # symbol.

As you can see, the block of code added to the htaccess file begins with:

BEGIN All In One WP Security

...and ends with:

END All In One WP Security

```
Require not env bad_bot
</RequireAll>
</IfModule>
</IfModule>
#AIOWPS_SIX_G_BLACKLIST_END
# END All In One WP Security
```

Another way to try and recover your site is by reinstating your .htaccess file by deleting all the plugin content. This is the code that starts with the opening **# BEGIN All In One WP Security** and ends with **# END All in One WP Security**. Make sure you save the edited file back to your server.

This should remove all security measures applied by the plugin.

If you don't want to manually edit this file, then simply restore the backup.

To do this:

1. Upload your backup to the root folder of your website.
2. Delete the original.
3. Rename your backup (which will have a random name created during its backup) to .htaccess.

If you are not sure which is the root folder of your site, you can quickly identify it because it contains these three WordPress folders:

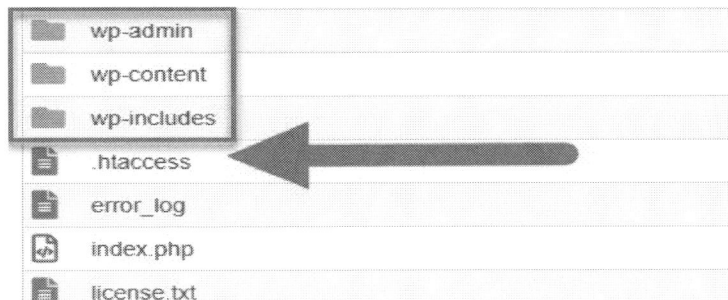

You can also see the original .htaccess file in the root folder. For Mac users, the .htaccess file is probably invisible by default, so you'll need to unhide it to see it.

After you restore the backup .htaccess file, you should have access to your site again through the regular login URL.

If you don't, you can use the same procedure to restore the wp-config.php file.

You should then get access back to your Dashboard. Now you can start to set up the plugin again.

Chapter 8 – Classification of Security Measures

To make things easier and safer, the plugin classifies its security measures into three categories:

1. Basic
2. Intermediate
3. Advanced

The **Basic** classification means it will not break your site.

The **Intermediate** classification means it can cause problems, but usually, it's fine.

The **Advanced** classification means be careful! This could break your site.

Our Security Strategy Going Forward

The best strategy is to activate all the basic measures immediately. These should be safe and will give your site a lot of protection against hackers.

After activating these, make a new backup of your files (the same ones as earlier). I suggest you save them to a separate folder (maybe call it "postbasic").

If you have to restore the files, you can use these "postbasic" ones. It's a simple system that means you won't have to configure the plugin again from scratch.

My advice is to test the site for a day or two to make sure everything works fine.

You can then go in and activate some of the intermediate measures and again take a backup of the files once you're done. Put these into a separate folder (maybe call this one "postinter").

Again, you'll test the site for a couple of days to make sure there are no issues.

You can then go in and activate some of the "advanced" features.

At any stage, if you have problems, you can go back and restore the files. Just choose the ones from the last working configuration before you implemented the advanced strategies.

In the next few chapters, we'll go through all the setup screens and most of the options: Basic, Intermediate, and Advanced. I'll tell you the settings I recommend you enable. Some of these will be Basic, some Intermediate, and a few Advanced.

The first time you go through these chapters, only activate the basic features I suggest. Once activated and working fine, backup the files and work through the chapters again. This time, enable my recommended "Intermediate" features. After a day or two, back up the files and work your way through these chapters again.

This time you'll enable my recommended "Advanced" features. This is our strategy.

There are a couple of settings that I know cause issues for some people. These can trigger the

IP lockouts we looked at earlier. I'll highlight those for you as we go through the settings. If the system locks you out, once you get access again, go and disable the known troublemakers first. Then log out of your site and back in again. You can then start to re-enable these settings one at a time and test them for a day or two before moving on.

OK, let's begin by looking at the Dashboard screen.

Chapter 9 – The Dashboard

If you click on **Dashboard** in the **WP Security** menu, the Dashboard screen loads. Across the top, as with many of these settings pages, you'll see a few tabs:

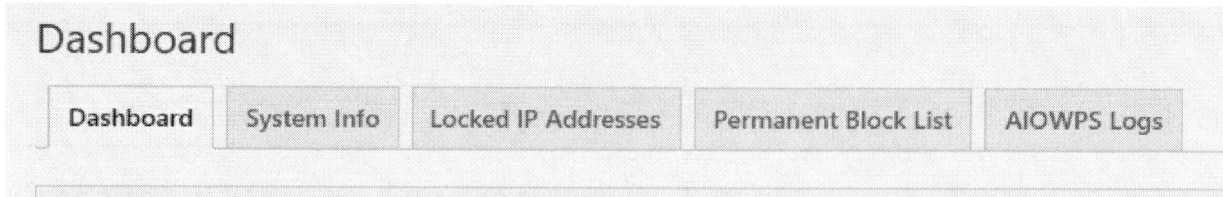

Dashboard

| Dashboard | System Info | Locked IP Addresses | Permanent Block List | AIOWPS Logs |

Here we have the Dashboard tab selected. From this tab, you can see the two graphical representations of your current security strength.

The first one is a dial, from zero to 515.

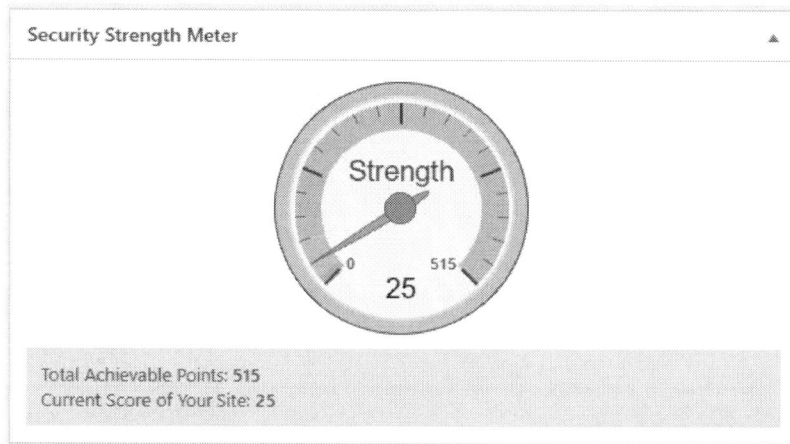

Security Strength Meter ▲

Strength

0   515
25

Total Achievable Points: 515
Current Score of Your Site: 25

515 is the maximum achievable score, though you won't get that high. At the 6 o'clock position, you can see my current score of 25.

The other graphic on this page is a pie chart. This includes a few segments that represent the security measures currently in force.

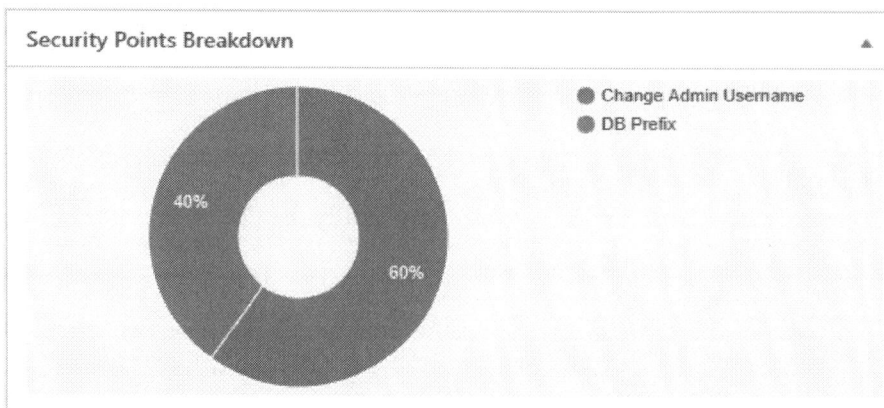

Security Points Breakdown ▲

● Change Admin Username
● DB Prefix

40%

60%

This pie chart gets more cluttered as you add extra security measures to your site.

Before you start, I recommend you record your security strength meter score. You can then compare it to your score at the end of this book.

Have a look down at the other information on this Dashboard screen. An interesting item is the **Critical Feature Status**. This shows the enabled status for a few of the more critical features:

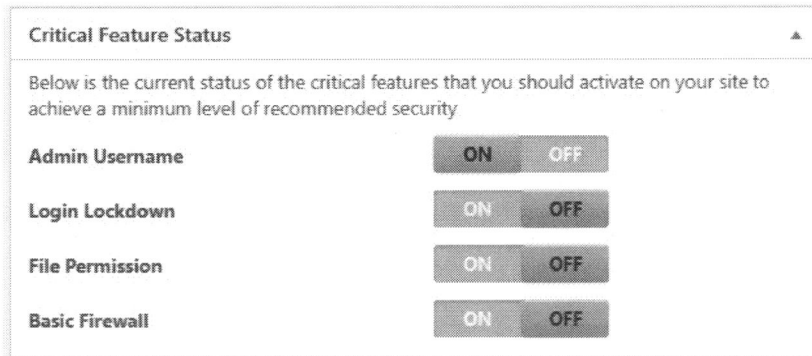

In my case, there's no login lockdown, file permissions need work, and I need to enable a basic firewall. These are three highly recommended security features.

You have two ways to activate these. The first is to use the sub-menus on the **WP Security** sidebar to access the correct settings page. For example, you'll find the basic firewall on the **Firewall** settings page.

A quicker way, though, is to simply click the "switch" on the **Critical Feature Status** panel. Do that now.

By clicking the **Login Lockdown** switch, the system automatically takes you to the settings page that contains the login lockdown feature.

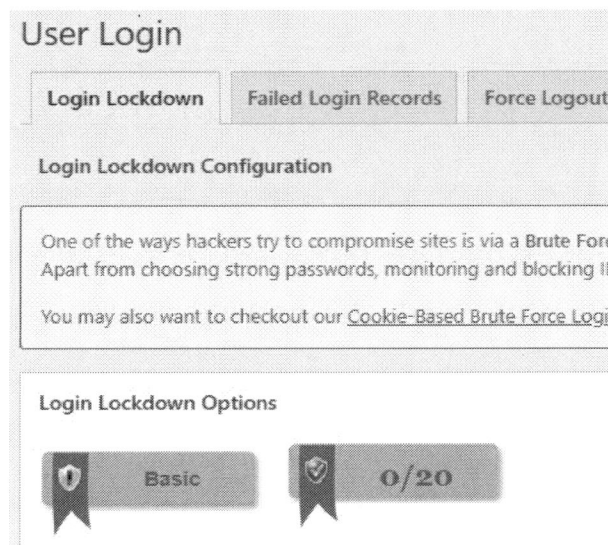

As you can see, this is on the **User Login** settings page, which you can also access from the main **WP Security** menu.

This screen also has tabs across the top, and we were taken to the **Login Lockdown** tab. This tab has a section called **Login Lockdown Options**. Currently, we score 0 out of a possible 20 points.

OK, let's set up the login lockdown.

The badge tells you this is a 'Basic' security measure. It means there's almost zero chance of it causing any issues. To activate the login lockdown, simply check the **Enable Login Lockdown Feature** box.

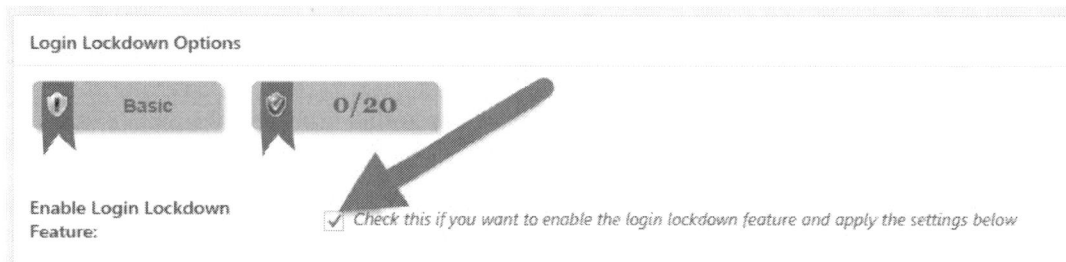

There are a few other options you can set up with this. I recommend you leave most of the other settings at their default values. There are helpful hints next to each checkbox if you want to know what each one does.

However, one setting I do recommend you edit is the **Instantly Lockout Specific Username**. Hackers often try the default "admin" username when they attempt to get access to your site. You should not be using that as a username. If you are, create a new admin user with a more secure username, then login with the new username and delete that "admin" username account. You won't lose any content created by that user because WordPress will ask you which user you want to move the content to.

OK, so you are not using **admin** as a username. Enter "admin" into the settings box:

If a hacker now attempts to get access using that username, they'll get blacklisted immediately.

Another item on that list you might want to think about is the **Max Login Attempts**. Ask yourself whether you frequently mistype the wrong username or password. If no, then you may want to reduce this from 3 to 2. Or set it to 1 if you use a password tool for entering passwords as there won't be any accidental login attempts. This setting tells the plugin when to lock a user out of your login page. If it's set to 1, when a visitor or hacker tries once and fails, the system automatically blocks their IP.

You can also specify how long you want to lock someone out before they can try again. Here, 60 minutes is the default and is probably a good time to use. This is plenty long enough to deter hackers. But it's short enough so that you don't lose a whole day of work if the system accidentally locks you out.

You can set up auto email notifications to inform you of any failed login attempts. Just enter an email address at the end of the form, and you're set.

At the bottom of the settings page, you can see a **Whitelist**. This is useful if you want to make sure a certain IP address always gets to login without issues. You can enter an IP address or range of IPs into the box. My advice is to only do this if you know what your IP will be every time you turn on your computer.

When you're happy with the settings, click the **Save Settings** button.

The **User Login** screen will reload, and you'll see you've scored 20 out of 20 for the login lockdown feature. Click on the **Dashboard** link to go back to the Dashboard.

Now recheck your security strength:

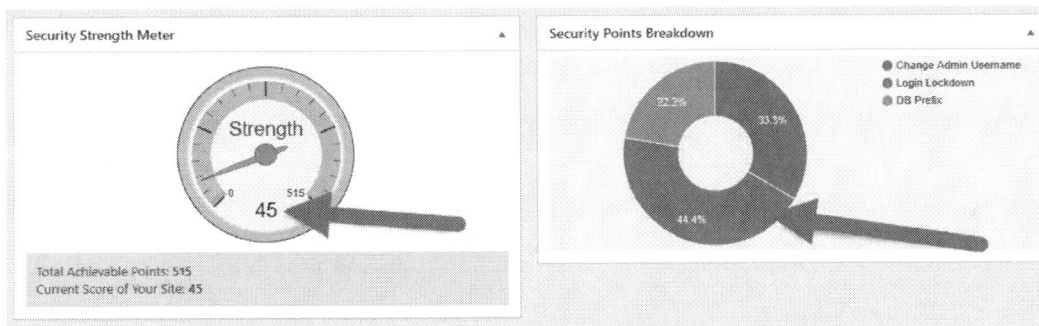

You can see how mine has increased by 20 points to 45. You can also see a new segment in the pie chart. I now have three security measures in place.

The next "critical" issue I need to fix is the **File Permission** feature.

Clicking that switch takes me to this screen:

There are two issues that can be fixed by clicking the **Set Recommended Permissions** button next to each item. This should then give you the all-clear!

Name	File/Folder	Current Permissions	Recommended Permissions	Recommended Action
root directory	/home/cheebles/public_html/	0755	0755	No Action Required
wp-includes/	/home/cheebles/public_html/wp-includes	0755	0755	No Action Required
.htaccess	/home/cheebles/public_html/.htaccess	0644	0644	No Action Required
wp-admin/index.php	/home/cheebles/public_html/wp-admin/index.php	0644	0644	No Action Required
wp-admin/js/	/home/cheebles/public_html/wp-admin/js/	0755	0755	No Action Required
wp-content/themes/	/home/cheebles/public_html/wp-content/themes	0755	0755	No Action Required
wp-content/plugins/	/home/cheebles/public_html/wp-content/plugins	0755	0755	No Action Required
wp-admin/	/home/cheebles/public_html/wp-admin	0755	0755	No Action Required
wp-content/	/home/cheebles/public_html/wp-content	0755	0755	No Action Required
wp-config.php	/home/cheebles/public_html/wp-config.php	0640	0640	No Action Required
Name	File/Folder	Current Permissions	Recommended Permissions	Recommended Action

Let's go back and see our security rating:

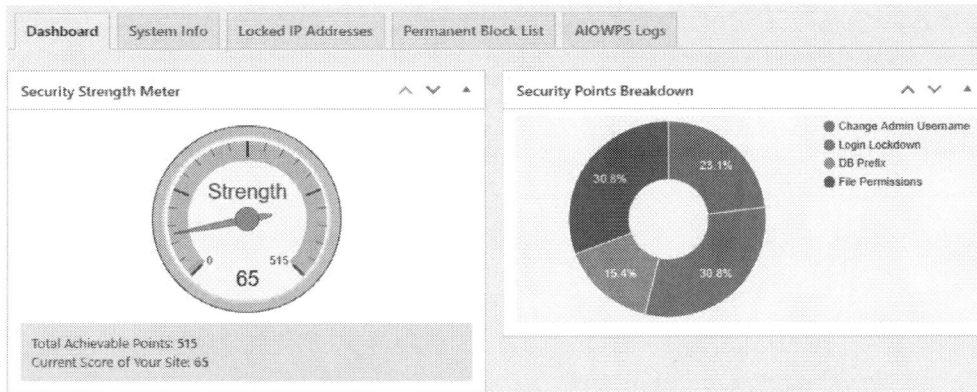

That has now gone up to 65 points, and the pie diagram has another slice.

The final "critical issue" from the **Critical Feature Status** we need to resolve is the **Basic Firewall:**

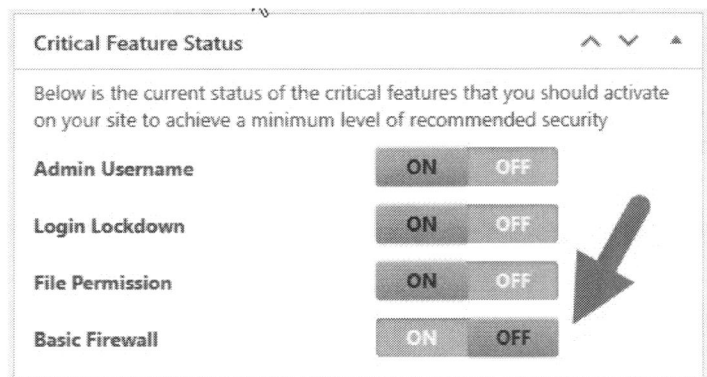

Click on the **Basic Firewall** switch to open the firewall settings:

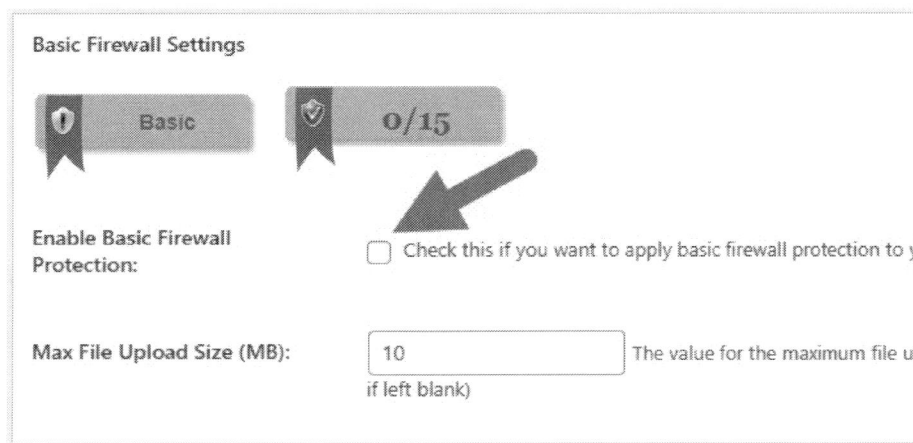

This screen has a few tabs across the top, and we'll come back to look at these later. For now, you can see my score for **Basic Firewall Settings** is 0 out of 15.

You can also see the "Basic" badge, so this setting is safe to use.

Check the box to enable the basic firewall. Now scroll to the bottom and click the **Save Basic**

Firewall Settings button.

Return to the Dashboard again to check your new security score:

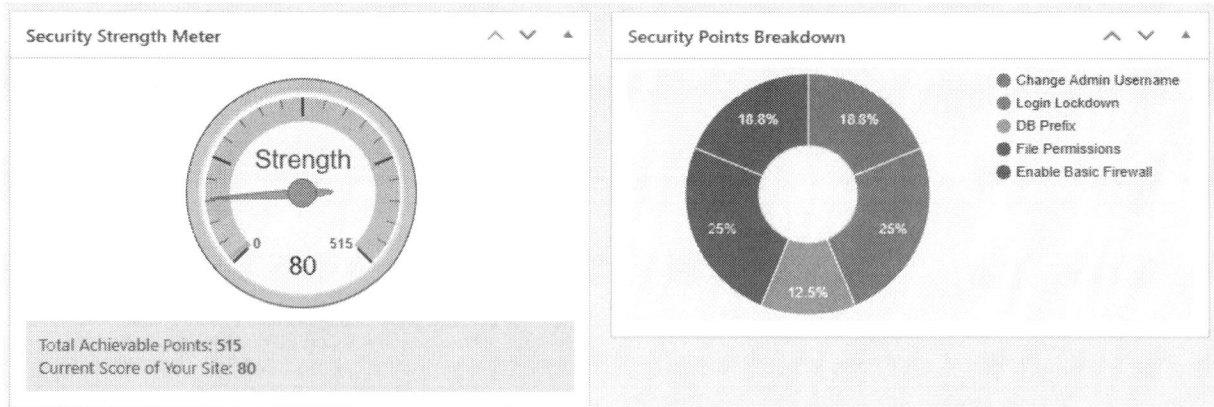

As you can see, with every new security measure you enable, the security on the site gets stronger.

There is one more thing I want to show you on the Dashboard tab. Look for the **Maintenance Mode Status** panel.

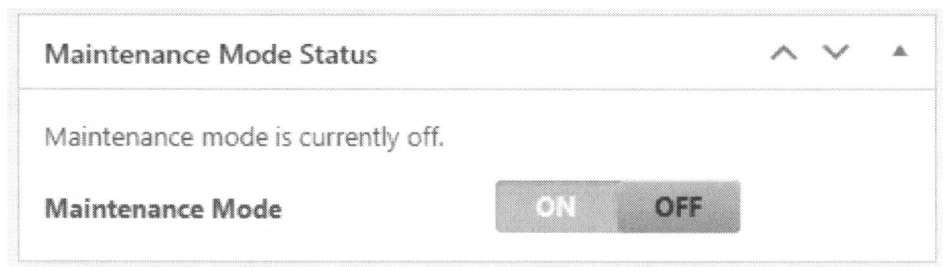

The current status is set to OFF, and you want to keep it off. Switching it "On" enables WordPress maintenance mode, and your site becomes unavailable to visitors.

Note: If you are logged in as an admin, you will still see your site as normal.

Visitors will get a message — something you can define yourself (we'll look at this again later in the book).

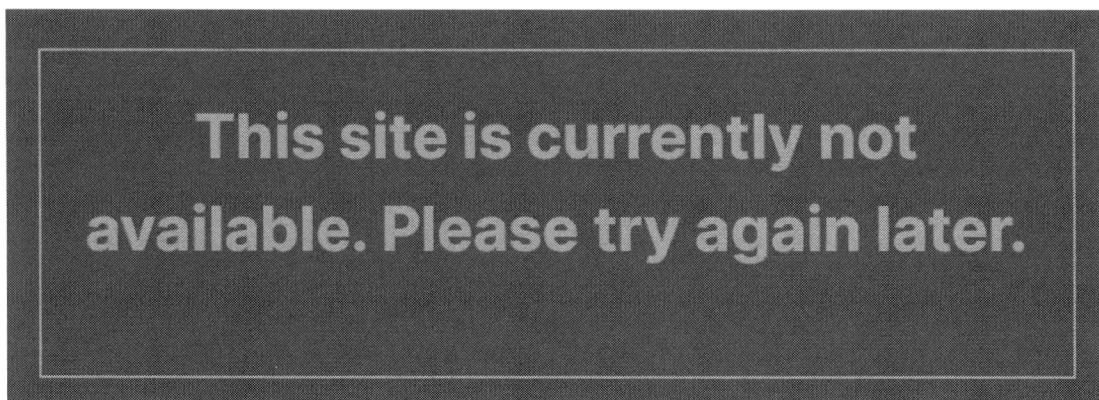

There may be times when you want to enable this, e.g., when you're doing work you don't want others to see. It's not something I've ever used, but you may find it useful.

OK, that's the Dashboard tab covered. You'll also see a few other tabs across the top. I won't go into details on these as we don't need them to set up your security. You can click on each one just to see what's there.

1. System Info

This provides some information about your website, server, and any software running on the server. For example, you may want to know what version of PHP your host is running. This screen gives you the information you need.

2. Locked IP Addresses

As the name suggests, this lists any current and temporarily locked out IP addresses. These would include any IP addresses locked out because of invalid login attempts.

3. Permanent Block list

This shows a list of all the permanently blocked IPs from your site.

4. AIOWPS Logs

AIOWPS stands for 'All In One WordPress Security.' This screen gives you access to any log files used by the plugin. You can examine them if you need to troubleshoot, for example. Most users won't ever need to look at these.

This concludes our **Dashboard** settings.

Chapter 10 – Settings

Click on **Settings** in the **WP Security** menu.

Earlier in the book, we created backups of important files. We created these backups using the **Settings** options. If you look at the tabs across the top of the **Settings** screen, you probably recognize them.

The **General Settings** tab provides links to back up the following:

1. Database
2. .htaccess file
3. Wp-config.php file

A useful feature on this screen is one we've not looked at yet. It's the **Disable All Security Features** button.

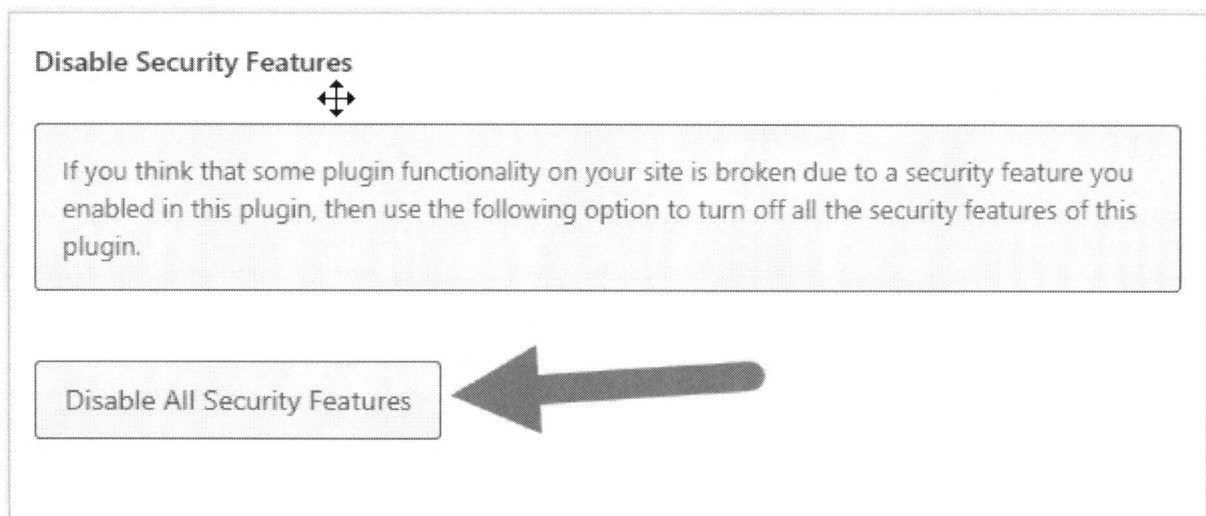

This button turns off all security measures enabled in the plugin. It's useful if you have problems with your site and can still log into the Dashboard. The killer switch resets all security measures back to their default settings. In my case, my security score would return to 25.

Another option you have here is to **Disable All Firewall Rules**. It's a less extreme measure to use if you think the issue relates to your firewall settings. It will delete all firewall settings from your site's .htaccess file and thus disable the firewall.

Finally, at the bottom of the screen is the **Debug Settings**. It turns on the debug mode and creates a log file, which can then help you to debug difficult situations. If your site is having stability issues, or you keep getting logged (or locked) out, enable the debug mode. This will store debug files in a "logs" folder inside the plugin folder on your server, so you can get access to these via FTP or cPanel.

The second tab on the **Settings** screen is the .htaccess file tab. This screen lets you back up your .htaccess file and restore one if you need to. If you can't log in to the Dashboard to restore the file, you can log in via FTP or File Manager in cPanel. It's then just a case of uploading the one you want to restore.

The wp-config.php tab allows you to backup and restore this file if necessary.

Now click on the **WP Version Info** tab.

One of the things hackers like to know is the version of WordPress you use for your site. If they know you're using version 5.1, for example, they can check what vulnerabilities exist with that particular version. They can then get to work and exploit those vulnerabilities. For some reason, WordPress likes to give this information out to anyone who wants it. They do this by including the info in the source code for every page on your site.

This plugin lets you remove that info by disabling the **WP Generator Meta Info**:

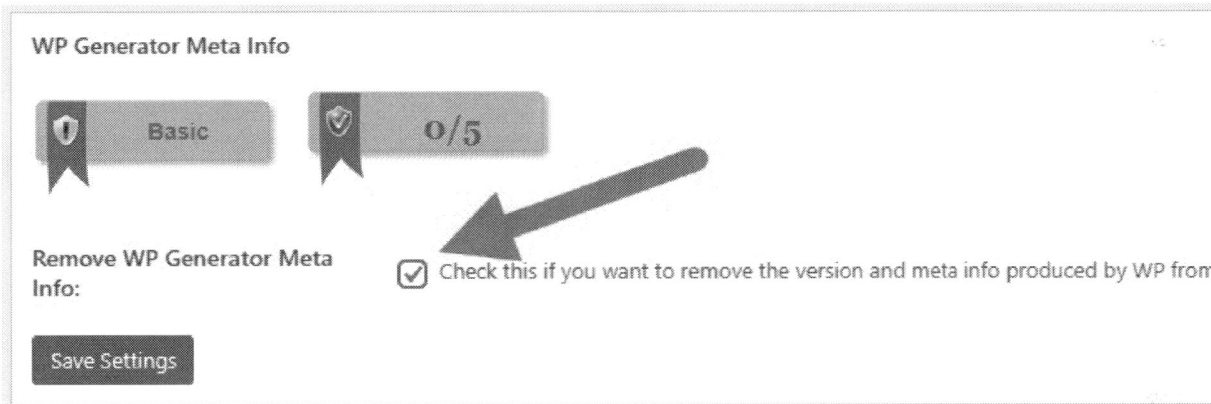

It's a "Basic" feature, so it's safe to implement. Check the box and click **Save Settings**. Your security score will go up by another 5 points.

The next tab is **Import/Export**. This allows you to export and import your security plugin settings. This is useful if you are setting up several sites and want to replicate the same security settings on all sites. Simply export from the site that is configured correctly, and then import those settings into all other sites. Of course, I do recommend you check any site that has imported settings, just to make sure everything is working as it should.

The final tab is for **Advanced Settings.**

This is an advanced feature that I don't recommend you change unless you know what you are doing. Essentially the plugin retrieves the IP addresses of your visitors - it needs to if it is going to block a hacker. This advanced settings tab allows you to define the method the plugin uses to retrieve those IP addresses. If you find that IP addresses are not being retrieved properly, you can switch to another method and test for reliability.

Chapter 11 – User Accounts

Click on the **User Accounts** link in the **WP Security** menu. You'll see three tabs.

The first tab is **WP Username**. This is a simple check to make sure you're not using "admin" as your username. If you are, you shouldn't be.

In my case, I'm not using "admin," but I've created a second user who does, just so I can show you what to expect. You can skip this setting if you already have 15 points for a non-admin username.

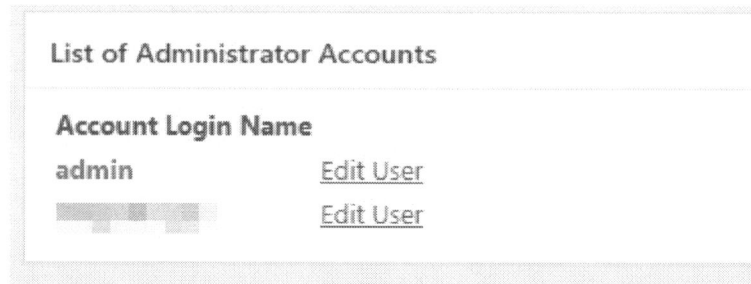

List of Administrator Accounts

Account Login Name

admin   Edit User

               Edit User

You can see two users in my demo (one blurred out).

I've logged in as the admin user, and further down the page I see this message:

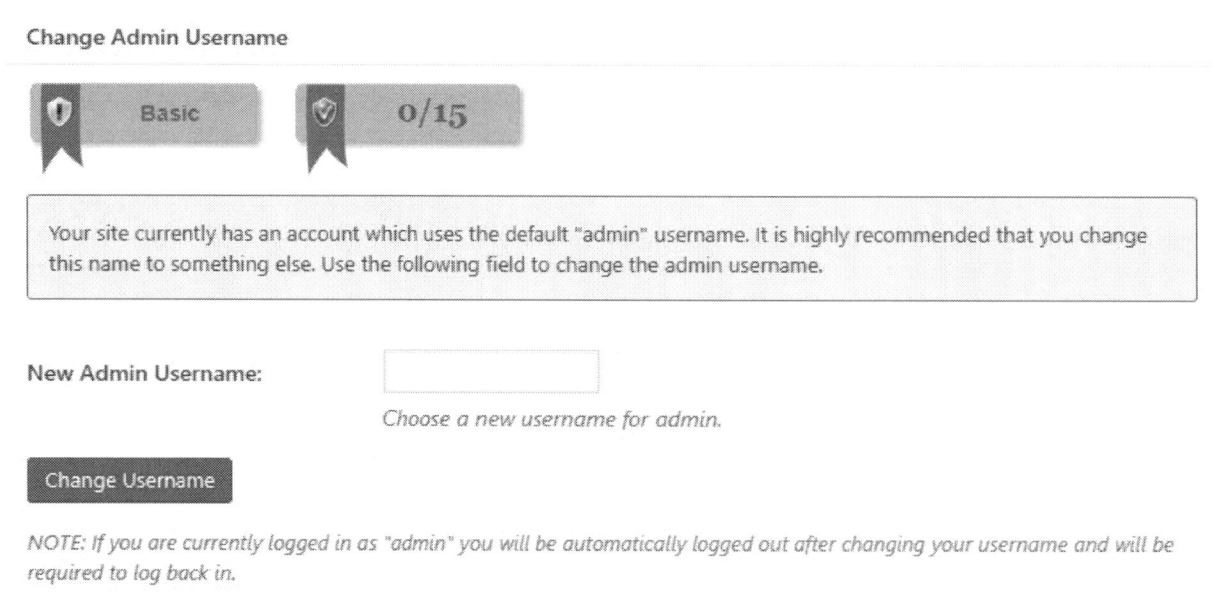

Change Admin Username

Basic   0/15

Your site currently has an account which uses the default "admin" username. It is highly recommended that you change this name to something else. Use the following field to change the admin username.

New Admin Username:

Choose a new username for admin.

Change Username

NOTE: If you are currently logged in as "admin" you will be automatically logged out after changing your username and will be required to log back in.

I get 0 out of 15 because my username is **admin**.

It's easy to change. I simply need to enter a new username in the box provided and then click **Change Username**.

The Dashboard then logs you out once you've changed your username.

Now you can log back in with your new username and old password.

You now get the 15 points allocated for a non-admin username.

The second tab on the **User Accounts** settings is **Display Name**. When you publish content on your site, WordPress displays your "nickname." Your nickname is your login name by default. This is a bad idea for security reasons because hackers know your username – one part of the login puzzle.

This setting in the plugin allows you to change your nickname (display name).

If your display name and username are the same, you get a warning:

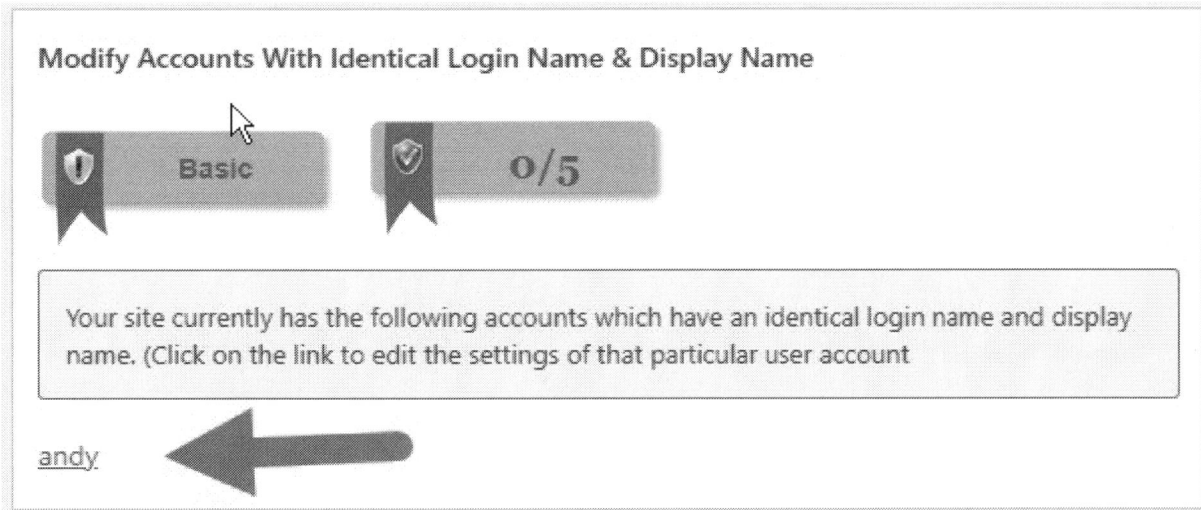

You can also see it's a "Basic" security measure, so it's safe to implement. At the moment, I've got a 0 score for this.

To change a display name, click the link of the username. The system then takes you to the profile page of the user. This is where you can select a different name in the **Display name publicly as** section:

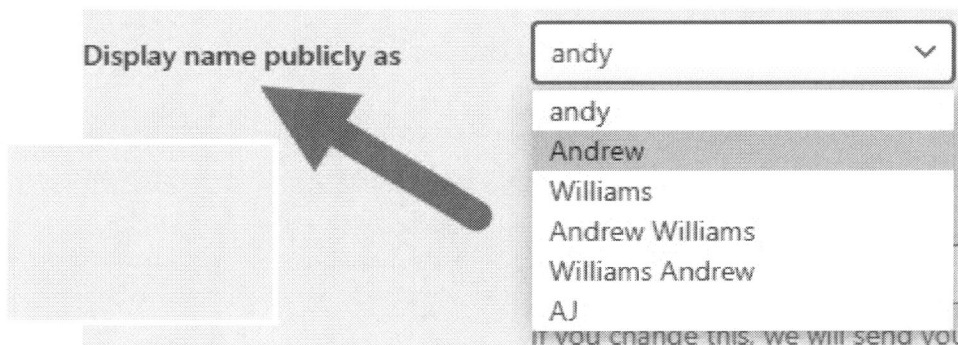

The **display name** options you have come from the fields: username, first name, last name, and nickname.

Select a name and then click **Update Profile**.

When you go back to the **User Accounts** settings, **Display Name** tab, you'll see 5/5:

Modify Accounts With Identical Login Name & Display Name

Basic   5/5

No action required.
Your site does not have a user account where the display name is identical to the username.

The final tab in the **User Account** settings is **Password**.

The password setting is not for changing your password but to check its strength. Use this tool to see if your password needs to be stronger (see image):

password

Start typing password.

It would take a desktop PC approximately
1 minute, 13 seconds
to crack your password!

Password
Strength

That's the **User Accounts** settings complete.

Back in the Dashboard, my security score has now gone up to 90, and the pie chart is starting to look a little more impressive.

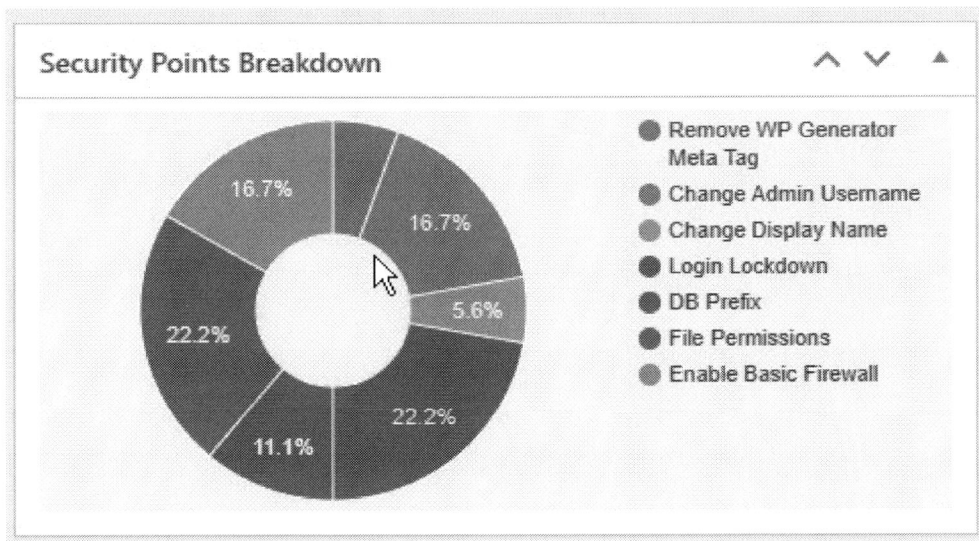

There's still a long way to go, though.

Chapter 12 – User Login

The next settings page is the **User Login** screen. This comes with a few useful tabs across the top:

User Login

| Login Lockdown | Failed Login Records | Force Logout | Account Activity Logs | Logged In Users |

The first tab is one we visited earlier – **Login Lockdown**. We've already configured those settings. There's another option I want to highlight, and that's the ability to lock out usernames.

It's interesting when you start to get information about who's trying to hack into your website. You can see how hackers attempt all manner of usernames to gain access. A lot of them will try "admin," but they'll try a lot of other educated guesses too. The best defense here is to lock out invalid usernames.

This plugin gives us that opportunity.

Instantly Lockout Invalid Usernames:

☑ Check this if you want to instantly lockout login attempts with usernames which do not exist on your system

Check the box to **Instantly Lockout Invalid Usernames**. Then, if someone tries to login with a username that doesn't correspond to a real user, they're blocked.

We saw earlier how we could lock out hackers that try to use the "admin" username. However, with a tick in the above checkbox, you don't need to worry about individual usernames, so you can delete "admin" from that box.

The next tab is the **Failed Login Records** screen. This one shows you a list of all failed logins on your site (mostly hacking attempts). Here are the failed login records for one of my other WordPress websites:

Failed Login Records

Login IP Range	User ID	Username	Date
2a02:...942a:...	...b2d		2...
119.73.113.178	0	ezseonews	2020-11-03 10:12:50
173.236.146.9	3	andy	2020-11-03 09:50:42
5.182.211.238	3	andy	2020-11-03 09:34:57
103.129.37.60	0	ezseonews	2020-11-03 09:32:49
34.73.10.30	3	andy	2020-11-03 09:17:27

Bulk Actions ∨ Apply

5,000 items « ‹ 1 of 50 ›

Search

The screenshot here shows 5,000 failed login attempts.

With each record, you can see the IP address of the user who tried to access my site. If the same IP crops up a lot, you can permanently block it if you want to.

You can also see the username exploited by the would-be hacker. In those three instances, they tried to use my first name, and in two others, the name of my site. See how important it's to change it?"

The next tab is **Force Logout**. It's a "Basic" security measure so we can enable it right away:

Force User Logout Options

Basic   5/5

Enable Force WP User Logout: ☑ Check this if you want to force a wp user to be logged out after a config

Logout the WP User After XX Minutes: 60 (Minutes) The user will be forced to log back in after this time

Save Settings

Force Logout logs out an admin user after they've been in the Dashboard for X minutes (60 minutes is the default). This can be useful because if a hacker gets in by chance, the system logs them out after the set period. If you don't usually spend long in your Dashboard, you can reduce the 60-minute limit still further. It's handy because it reduces the time a hacker has to wreak havoc on your site.

Remember, the system logs you out after this time too. If it becomes a nuisance, you may want to leave the feature disabled.

If you do enable it, make sure you click the **Save Settings** button.

The **Account Activity Logs** screen displays the activity of registered accounts in your Dashboard. It shows you the last 50 logins, with username, IP, and timestamp. You should be able to recognize all of these users.

The final tab is the **Logged in Users**. It simply shows you the users logged into your Dashboard right now. You can see the login name and IP address. It's for information only.

Chapter 13 – User Registration

The **User Registration** settings are only important if you allow visitors to register on the site. If that is the case, make sure you manually approve all new users. This is a basic security measure.

On the **User Registration** screen:

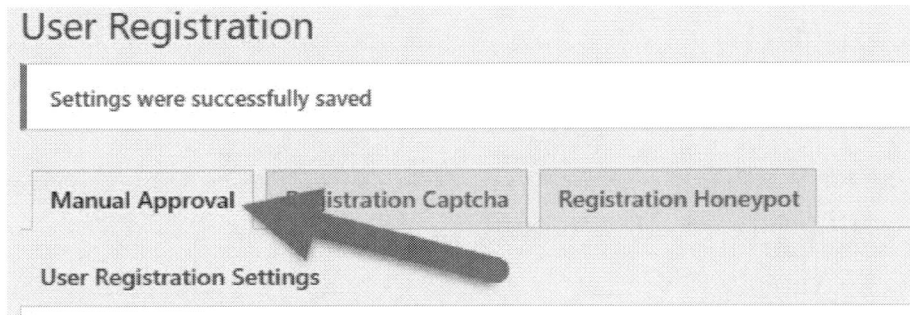

Go to the **Manual Approval** tab and check the **Enable manual approval of new registrations** checkbox. Now click **Save Settings**.

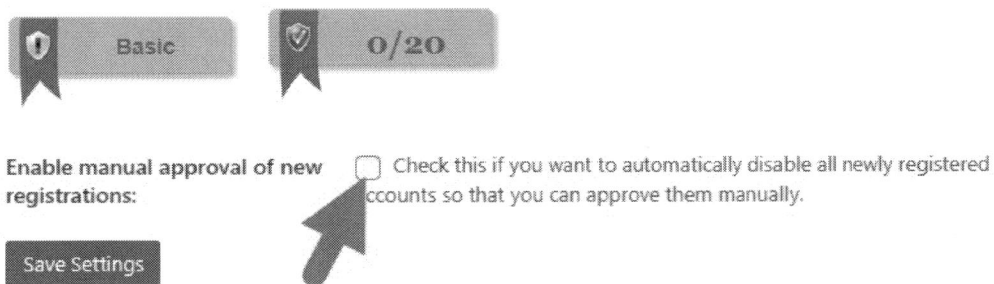

You can also enable a Captcha on the user registration form. This helps to cut down on automated bot registrations. To activate the Captcha (another basic setting), click on the **Registration Captcha** tab. Check the box to **Enable Captcha on Registration Page**:

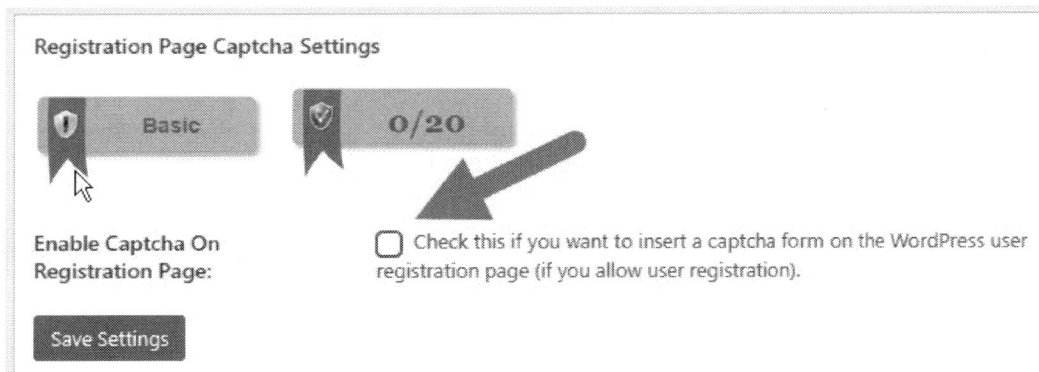

Click the **Save Settings** button.

Finally, there's an "Intermediate" security measure on the **Registration Honeypot** tab.

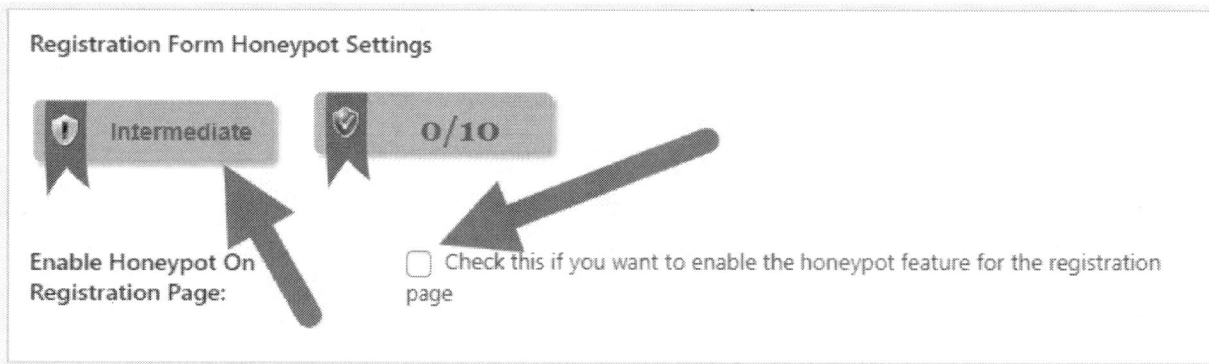

Registration Form Honeypot Settings

Intermediate   0/10

Enable Honeypot On Registration Page: ☐ Check this if you want to enable the honeypot feature for the registration page

This feature adds a hidden field (honeypot) on the registration page that is not seen by real humans but is visible to bots. When a bot comes along and fills in the form, including the honeypot field, the plugin knows it is not a real human and blocks the attempt.

Since this is an "Intermediate" feature, you need to be careful when implementing it. As I mentioned earlier in the book, I recommend you only activate basic features the first time around. Once you're certain they're working properly, go back and activate the "Intermediate" features.

When you're done, make sure you **Save Settings**.

Chapter 14 – Database Security

The **Database Security** screen has two tabs: the **DB Prefix** and **DB Backup** screens.

On the DB Prefix screen, you can make sure your database doesn't use the old default wp_ as a prefix on your databases. If you've installed WordPress recently, you should be fine. An automated installer like Softaculous will create a random prefix at the install stage.

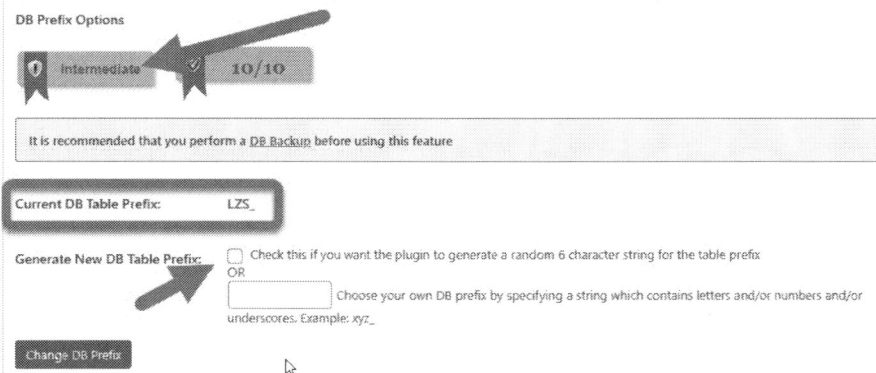

This is an "Intermediate" feature. That means it could cause some issues. If you use the plugin to change the prefix (and only do it if your prefix is wp_), there's a slim chance it might corrupt your database. I've never had a problem with this, and I suspect you won't either, but it's potentially problematic. As you can see, my prefix is a random one, so I don't need to change this.

To be safe, there's a link for the **DB Backup** feature. I recommend you backup now, even if you only intend to activate basic features at this point. It's a good habit to get into, and backing up healthy files never hurt any site.

Once done, check the box to **Generate New DB Table Prefix** and click the **Change DB Prefix** button.

You should see a confirmation message to inform you everything went smoothly:

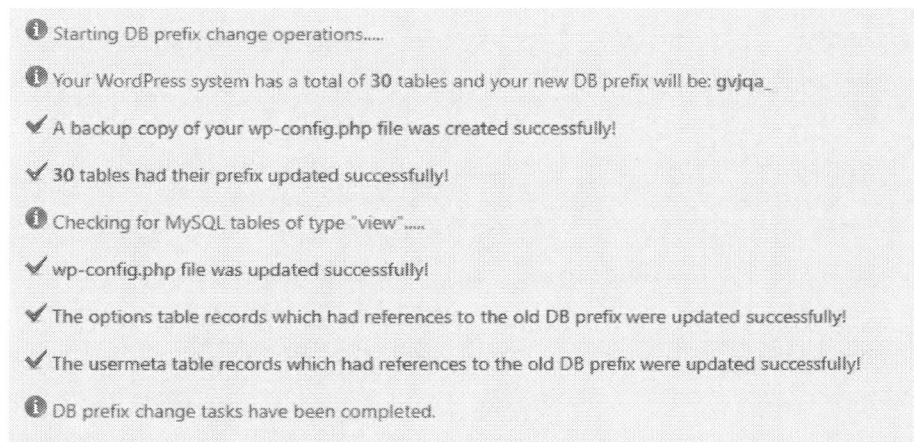

The other tab on the **Database Security** settings has the tools for backing up the database. At the top, you can see an option to manually back up the database:

Below is something really useful—an automated backup tool. This is a "Basic" security measure and adds 20 points to your score. If you have already set up Updraft Plus to take backups, you don't need this, though you may still enable it if you want.

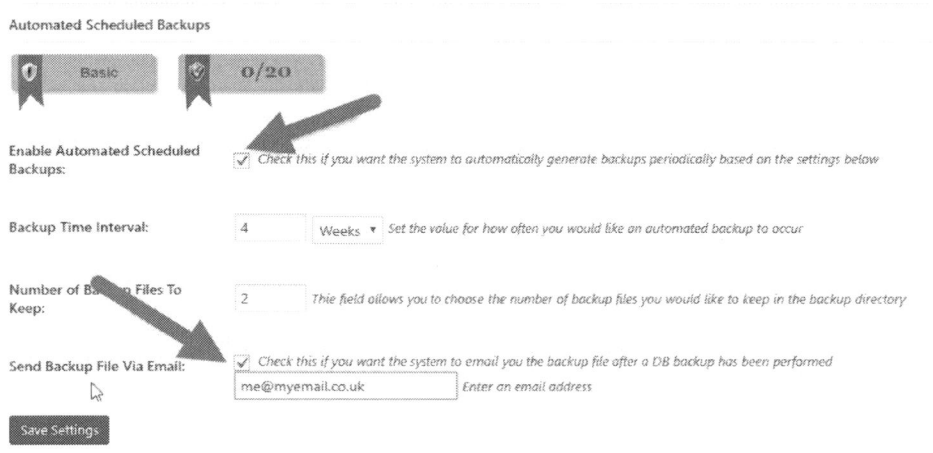

Check the box to **Enable Automated Scheduled Backups.**

You can choose how often to create backups. If you work a lot on your site, you might want weekly backups. The default is every four weeks, and that's fine for a site that doesn't add much new content each month.

You can specify how many backups to keep. The default is two, but I'd push that up to three.

Finally, if you want the backups emailed to you, check the box at the bottom and enter the email address you want to use.

Click **Save Settings** when you're done.

Now go back and check your security strength. Mine is now up to 155.

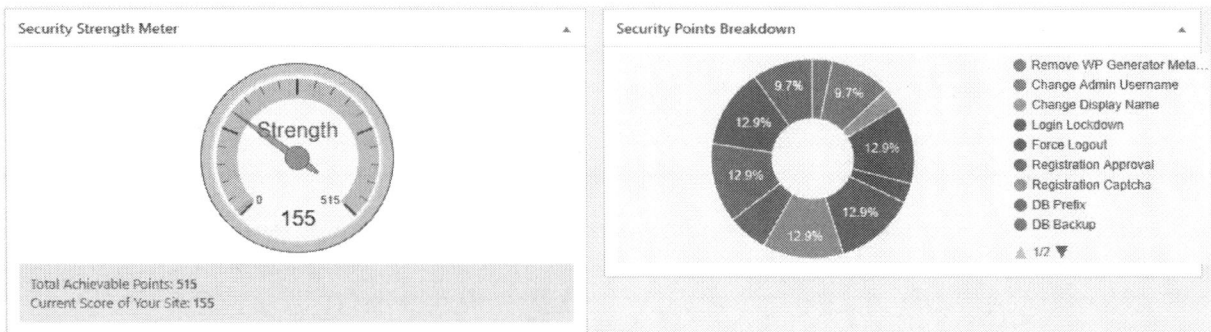

Chapter 15 – Filesystem Security

The **Filesystem Security** settings check to make sure the files and folders use the correct permissions. Remember, it's important to restrict access to your files and folders to only those systems and people who need access.

There are four tabs on the **Filesystem Security** screen.

File Permissions is the first tab. Here you'll see a table of files and folders, together with their current and recommended permissions.

We saw this earlier when we fixed **Critical Feature Status** items (remember those "switches"?).

In the table above, you can see the root directory of the site has permissions of 0750, but the plugin recommends 0755. You can check what this means by referring to the section earlier in the book where we discussed these numbers.

This permission setting is not a big security threat (you can see we already have 20 out of 20), but we'll fix it anyway. We can do this by clicking the **Set Recommended Permissions** button next to that entry in the table. This is what I get:

AIOWPS has corrected the permissions for me with a single click.

Once you've corrected permissions on your site, click the **PHP File Editing** tab.

When a hacker breaks into your Dashboard, one of the first places they go is the PHP file editor. With this tool, they can hack into the plugin and theme files. They can then change them or inject malicious code into the files.

A simple way to prevent this is to disable the PHP editor. If you — as a webmaster — want to edit the PHP files at any time, you still can. All you do is access the files via FTP or File Manager in cPanel, so it's no big deal.

This is a "Basic" security measure, so it's safe to do now.

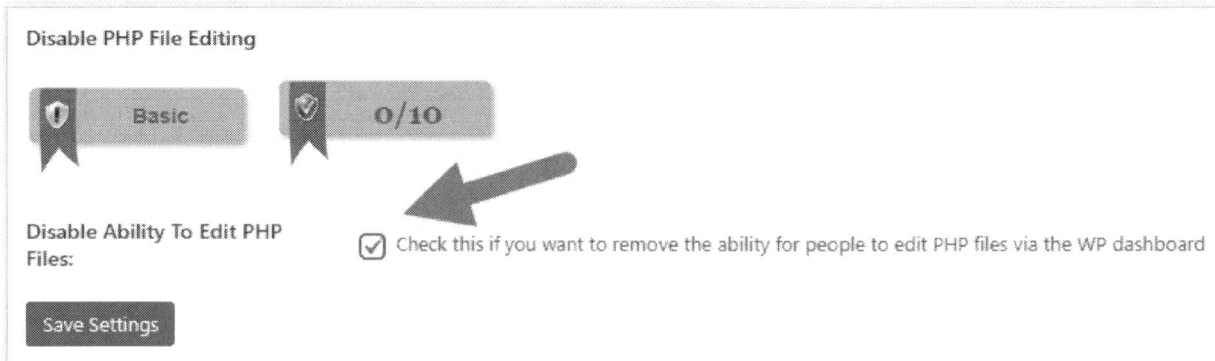

Simply check the box to **Disable Ability to Edit PHP Files** and click **Save Settings.**

Now click on the **WP File Access** tab. This tab allows you to hide other files that a hacker might use to gain information about your site.

Again, it's a "Basic" security measure and, therefore, safe to implement right away.

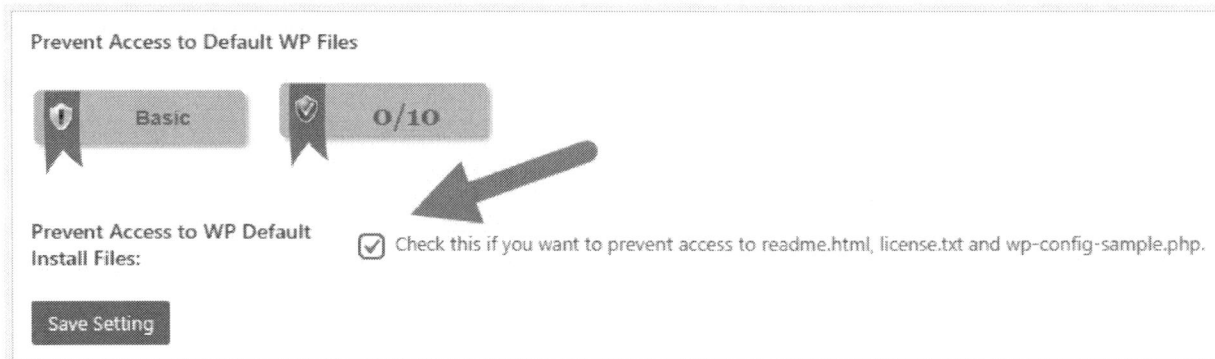

Check the box to **Prevent Access to WP Default Install Files. **Click **Save Settings**.

The final tab in these settings is the **Host System Logs**. This tab allows you to view your hosting error log files. You'll need to know the name of the files produced by your hosting server to make use of this feature.

Chapter 16 – Blacklist Manager

This is a really useful tool because it allows you to block IP addresses from accessing your site.

Click on the **Blacklist Manager** on the sidebar menu.

At the top of the page, you'll see something like this:

You may also be interested in our Country Blocking Addon.
This addon allows you to automatically block IP addresses based on their country of origin.

The plugin can block specific IP addresses, but that's not all. The **Country Blocking Addon** allows you to block entire countries if you need to. That plugin is a paid upgrade, though, and I don't cover it in this book.

You'll also notice that this security feature is an "Advanced" one. You need to use it with some caution. I recommend you activate this at a later date once you're sure everything else is working fine. If you misuse this feature, you could find yourself locked out of your site.

To activate the blacklist, check the **Enable IP or User Agent Blacklisting** box.

You can now enter the IP address(es) you want to block. You can use a wildcard to specify a range, e.g., 31.184.238.* This blocks out all IP addresses that start with 31.184.238.

You can also enter full IP addresses:

Enter IP Addresses:

31.184.238.*
52.166.125.125

When you enter a new IP address, make sure you put each one on a separate line.

You can also block user agents. This includes all kinds of bots that roam the internet, e.g., baiduspider, SurveyBot, and so on.

Enter User Agents:

baiduspider
SquigglebotBot

You block these by entering their names in the second box.

Chapter 17 – Firewall

We activated the basic firewall when we first installed the plugin. There're a lot more firewall settings you can activate. Some are Basic, and others are Intermediate or Advanced. Let's go through each of these.

Click on the **Firewall** menu in the left sidebar.

You'll see the firewall screen has a few tabs across the top. For now, you should be on the **Basic Firewall Rules** tab.

At the top, you can see the basic firewall enabled (we did that earlier).

Below this is another "Basic" feature:

WordPress XMLRPC & Pingback Vulnerability Protection

⚠ Basic	✓ 0/15

Completely Block Access To XMLRPC:	☐ *Check this if you are not using the WP XML-RPC functionality and* + More Info
Disable Pingback Functionality From XMLRPC:	☐ *If you use Jetpack or WP iOS or other apps which need WP XML-RP* *WordPress pingback vulnerabilities.* + More Info

Point to note: Before you activate this feature, you need to read a little further.

The first option is to **Completely Block Access to XMLRPC**. The thing is, you may need XMLRPC functionality, so disabling it could cause you problems. On the other side of the coin, XMLRPC is a common gateway for hackers. If you're not using it, I suggest you disable it.

Example: I use Open Live Writer (previously Windows Live Writer) to manage my blog content. It's a tool I use for writing content offline. When I'm ready, I then publish the post direct from within Open Live Writer. This tool requires XMLRPC to function. To disable it would stop Open Live Writer from working. In short, I wouldn't be able to publish content to the site because the program would no longer connect.

Another example is the Jetpack plugin. This requires XMLRPC as well. Fortunately, the plugin gives you an easy way around this problem. You can tell it that you use Jetpack or any other apps that need XMLRPC to work.

You have two options.

If you want to completely block XMLRPC, check the **Completely Block Access to XMLRPC** box. This overwrites the **Disable Pingback Functionality From XMLRPC** feature, so it doesn't matter what you do with that checkbox, it'll be ignored.

The second option is to allow software and plugins that need XMLRPC but to block anything else. To achieve this, check the **Disable Pingback Functionality From XMLRPC.** Make sure the **Completely Block Access to XMLRPC** box is UNCHECKED:

WordPress XMLRPC & Pingback Vulnerability Protection

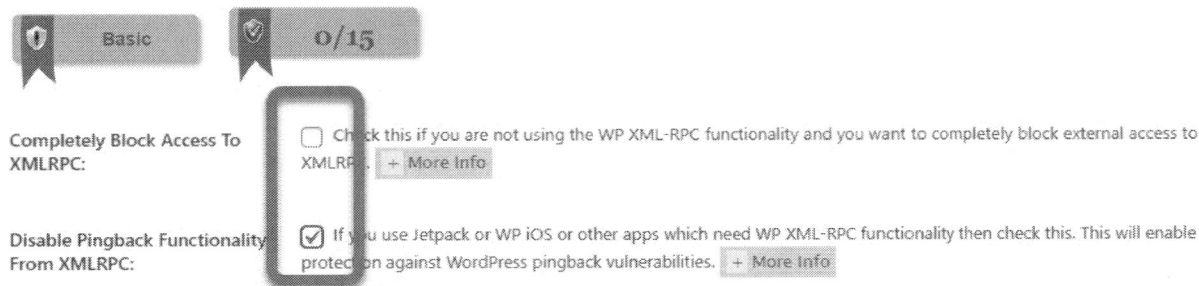

Basic	0/15

Completely Block Access To XMLRPC: ☐ Check this if you are not using the WP XML-RPC functionality and you want to completely block external access to XMLRPC. + More Info

Disable Pingback Functionality From XMLRPC: ☑ If you use Jetpack or WP iOS or other apps which need WP XML-RPC functionality then check this. This will enable protection against WordPress pingback vulnerabilities. + More Info

The final feature on the basic firewall rules tab is **Block Access to Debug Log File.**

This is an "Intermediate" feature that prevents access to a debug log file. This file can contain sensitive information, so I recommend you eventually enable it.

When you're done with the basic rules, click on the **Additional Firewall Rules** tab.

These features are all "Intermediate" or "Advanced." I suggest you come back and activate these once you're sure your basic settings are behaving well.

The first option is to **Listing of Directory Content.** Some web servers allow the listing of files and folders in the webspace. This isn't a great idea as it gives hackers more information about your site. My advice is to enable this feature:

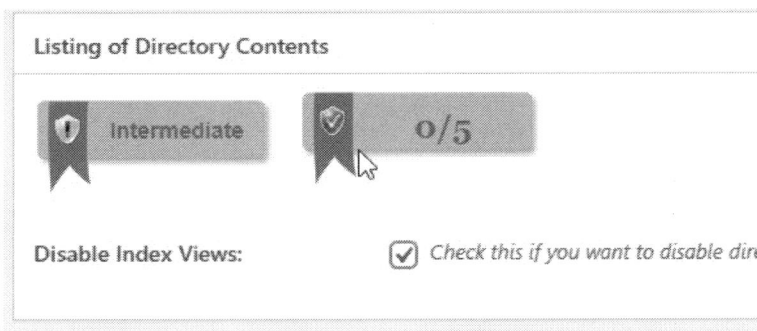

Listing of Directory Contents

Intermediate	0/5

Disable Index Views: ☑ Check this if you want to disable dire

The next option lets you disable trace and track. This will prevent what's called an HTTP Trace attack.

I recommend you enable it—eventually—but it's an "Advanced" security measure, so leave it for the time being.

Next up is another "Advanced" option, but it's an important one that helps to cut down on spam. The **Proxy Comment Posting** option allows you to block comments coming in from a proxy server (used by people trying to hide their true IP address). I recommend you enable this option—eventually.

The next option is **Bad Query Strings**. You need to be careful with this one, though. Activating it may cause conflicts with certain plugins or themes. Make sure you backup your .htaccess file before you implement it. This way, you can quickly revert if there's an issue.

The final option on this screen is the **Advanced Character String Filter**. This feature can help prevent Cross-Site Scripting attacks (XSS). Once again, it's an "advanced" feature and can break your site. Take a backup of your .htaccess file before you implement it.

When you're done, click on the **Save Additional Firewall Settings** button.

You can now go over to the **6G Blacklist Firewall Rules** tab.

When you decide to activate "Advanced" measures, I recommend you activate the 6G firewall protection on this screen:

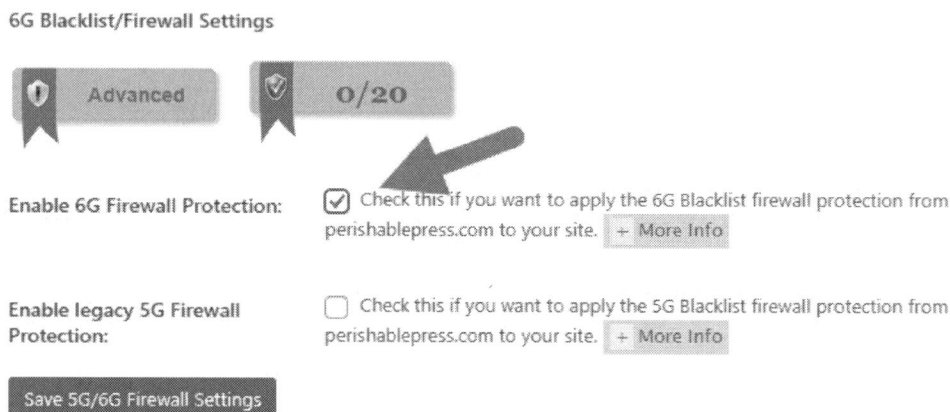

Don't bother with the 5G. That's an older form of protection that the 6G firewall has since replaced.

The next tab in the **Firewall** settings is the **Internet Bots** tab.

This is an "Advanced" feature that aims to block malicious bots masquerading as Googlebot:

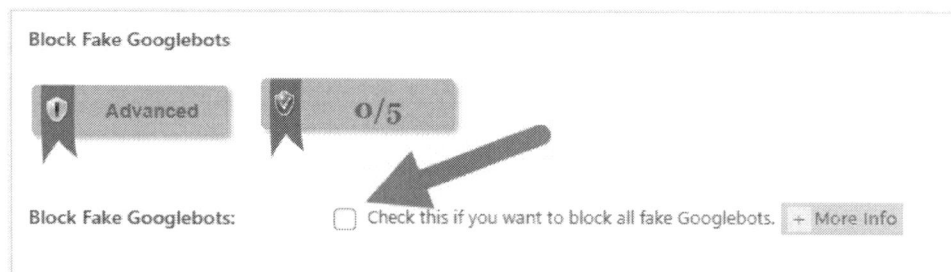

I recommend you eventually activate it. The plugin will then perform verification tests on any bot claiming to come from Google and block those that fail the tests.

OK, now save your settings and move onto the **Prevent Hotlinks** tab.

If you have images on your site, each one will have its own URL. Anyone can grab the URLs of your images and embed them into their own site. It's a problem not least because YOUR server serves the image wherever they are. So, every time the rogue site loads one of your stolen images, it uses YOUR bandwidth.

For this reason, I recommend you activate this "Basic" feature:

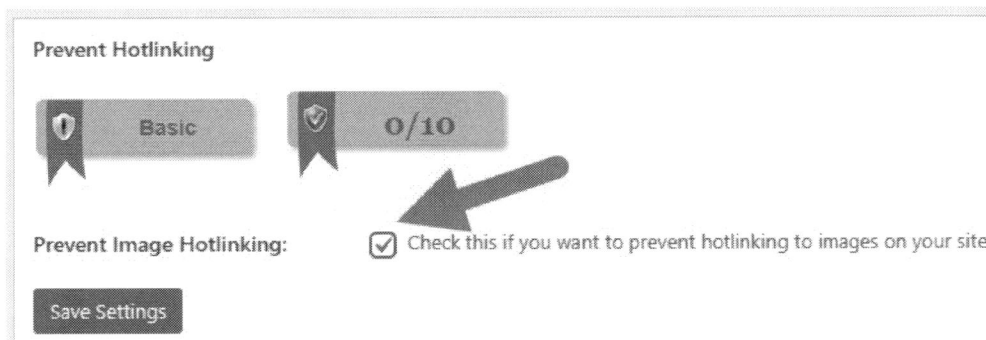

Save the settings, then click on the **404 Detection** tab.

When a visitor tries to view a page on your site that no longer exists, they'll likely see a 404 error. The message explains that the page they're looking for is no longer available. It's correct, and the way websites should function. Real visitors can innocently get to 404 pages via broken links. For example, a link that points to a page the webmaster has since moved or deleted.

The difference with hackers is that they try lots of web pages in a short space of time as they search for a download page. They'll likely come across a series of 404 errors in a matter of minutes or seconds even. This identifies them as hackers, and it's what this feature aims to do. Identify hackers and then block them.

This is an "Intermediate" feature, but I recommend you enable it—eventually.

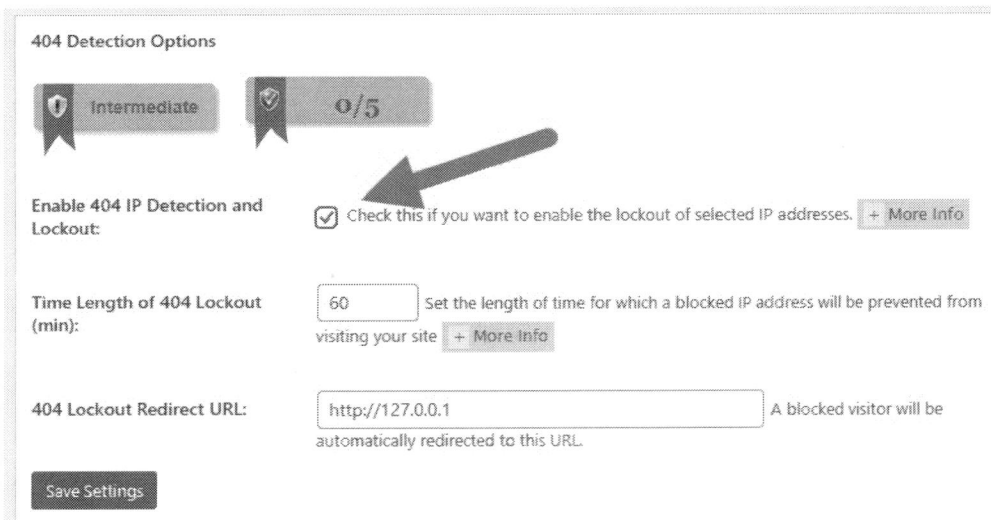

To enable, check the **Enable 404 IP Detection and Lockout** box and leave the other settings as they are. When the plugin identifies a hacker, it sends them to the 404 Lockout Redirect URL. You can enter anything you want in that box or just leave it at the default. It's completely up to you.

When you do eventually enable it, remember that it is enabled in case you keep getting directed to the **404 Lockout Redirect URL.**

If the system locks someone out with this security measure, you'll see the details of these events in the **404 Event Logs** on this screen.

Here are the logs for one of my sites:

If you find any repeat IP addresses in the list, especially if the events are within seconds of each other, you know you've found a bot. Any repeat IP addresses are good candidates to add to the blacklist!

To block an IP, you can mouse-over the event ID to bring up a menu:

Here you get the option for a temporary block or to blacklist the IP address.

The final tab on the **Firewall** screen is for **Custom Rules.**

This is for anyone who wants to add custom rules to the .htaccess file. These advanced techniques are beyond the scope of this book and can easily break a site.

Chapter 18 – Brute Force Protection

The **Brute Force** settings will help prevent "brute force attacks" on your website.

In my experience, these settings cause website owners the biggest problems. They'll often lock the webmaster out of their Dashboard. If you get them to work well, though, they provide a serious and powerful layer of protection.

There are a couple of really useful options. The first one is to rename the WordPress login page so that scripts and bots can't find it.

The **Rename Login Page Settings** panel is where you can rename this page. It's an "Intermediate" feature, so take care.

Read the warning box at the top, and click the link to read the message. If your web host uses server caching, this feature could easily break your site.

To activate it, check the **Enable Rename Login Page Feature**. Next, enter a string of characters that are hard to guess in the **Login Page URL** box.

Save Settings once done. You must remember your new login page URL.

I don't activate this feature. Instead, I use the **Cookie Based Brute Force Prevention** method—your second option to prevent brute force attacks.

Click on the tab of the **Brute Force** settings.

This **Cookie Based Brute Force Prevention** method is an "Advanced" feature. If you run into problems, I suggest you deactivate it and use the login page renaming method instead.

Before you activate the cookie-based method, scroll to the bottom of the screen and click on the **Perform Cookie Test** button. It will check to make sure your system is capable of using this method of protection.

Hopefully, you should receive the following confirmation:

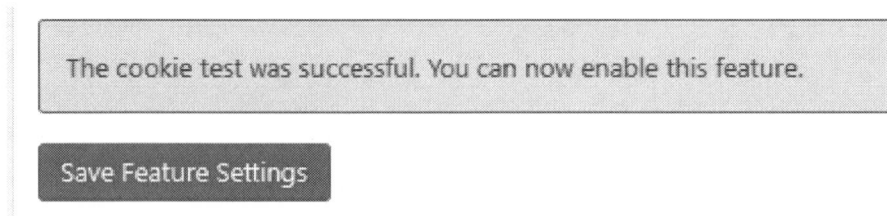

The cookie test was successful. You can now enable this feature.

Save Feature Settings

To enable this method, check the **Enable Brute Force Attacks Prevention** box. Now enter a secret word into the **Secret Word** box. It should be difficult to guess and will become part of your new login URL.

Does your website have any posts or pages that are password protected? If it does, make sure you check the **My Site Has Posts or Pages which are Password Protected** box.

If your WordPress theme or plugins use Ajax, check the **My Site Has a Theme or Plugins Which Use Ajax** box.

Now click on the **Save Feature Settings** box.

At the top of the screen, you'll see confirmation that your new login page is ready, and you'll see the URL. It should look something like the one below:

http://mysite.com/?mysecretword=1

You MUST copy and save that URL to a safe place. If you lose it, you won't be able to log into your Dashboard.

The way the protection works is to write a cookie to your computer when you visit that URL. That URL then redirects you to your login page. But if the cookie's not on your computer, you won't be able to log in, not even with the correct username and password.

Imagine a hacker comes to your login page. Even if they know your username and password, they still can't access your site if they haven't visited your secret URL first to pick up the cookie. That's pretty cool.

The next tab on the **Brute Force** settings is the **Login Captcha** screen.

You'll find three "Basic" features on this screen that you can activate if you want.

These put a captcha on the login form, custom login form, and lost password form, respectively.

Captchas can help reduce brute force attacks because logins require a mathematical problem to be solved.

Check all three boxes and save the settings.

The next tab is the **Login Whitelist** screen.

This screen lets you specify which IP addresses (or range of addresses) you allow logging into your Dashboard. If you use this feature, it'll block all other unspecified IP addresses. It's an "Intermediate" feature, so use it with caution. It works by writing directly to your .htaccess file, so back that up before you enable it.

I don't use this feature, and nor do I recommend you use it either unless you know what you're doing.

The last tab in the **Brute Force** settings is the **Honeypot**. This is a clever protection method that shows a hidden "honeypot" field on the login page to all bots. Human visitors don't see it, but bots do. They then fill in the "honeypot" field, and the plugin knows it's a bot.

This is an "Intermediate" measure, but I do recommend you enable it—eventually.

Chapter 19 – SPAM Prevention

Everybody hates comment spam. Fortunately, the All in One plugin includes a few features to help combat comment spam.

Click on **SPAM Prevention** in the WP Security sidebar menu.

There are four tabs across the top.

SPAM Prevention

| Comment SPAM | Comment SPAM IP Monitoring | BuddyPress | BBPress |

The first one is the **Comment Spam** settings.

One way to cut down on spam comments is to add a Captcha to the comment form. Captchas don't stop spammers from leaving comments, but they do make life more difficult and inconvenient for them, and that's a good thing. The **Add Captcha to Comments Form** option is a "Basic" feature, so it's safe to implement right away. For this, you'll get 20 more points towards your security score.

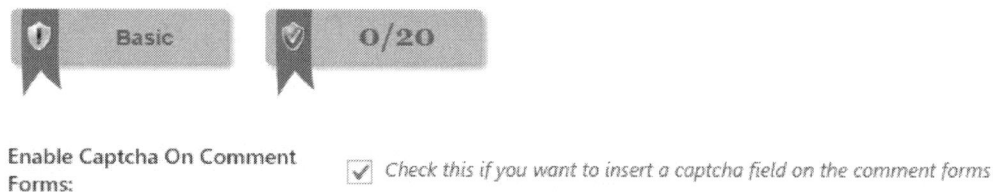

Basic   0/20

Enable Captcha On Comment Forms:

☑ Check this if you want to insert a captcha field on the comment forms

Once saved, your comment form will have something like this above the **Post Comment** button:

PLEASE ENTER AN ANSWER IN DIGITS:

eleven + fourteen =

POST COMMENT

This means a human will need to enter the answer for the comment to arrive in your pending list.

On the **Comment Spam** settings, there is also the option to **Block Spambots from Posting Comments**. Spambots are pieces of software that allow mass submission of comments to hundreds or thousands of sites in a very short space of time. This plugin can tell if it's a spambot trying to post because, unlike a real visitor, the request to post a comment won't originate from your domain. We can, therefore, block spambots from posting by checking the **Block Spambots from Posting Comments** checkbox.

Save settings before continuing.

The second tab on the **SPAM Prevention** settings is the **Comment SPAM IP Monitoring** settings.

When spam comments get into your site, you can approve them, send them to trash, or mark them as spam (get familiar with spam comments).

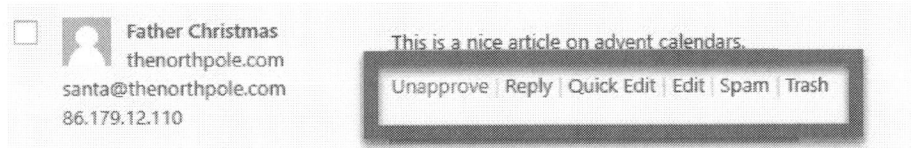

The Spam option is the one you should use. Together with this plugin, comments marked as spam can trigger an automatic block on the IP that posted it.

Here are the settings I recommend:

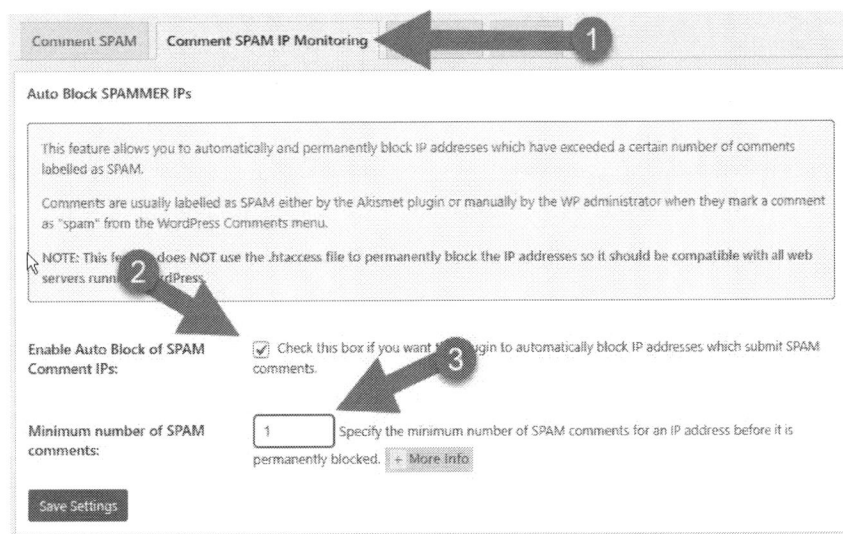

Whenever you mark a comment as spam in the future, the plugin will add the IP address of the sender to the blocked IP list. The reason I choose 1 for the "minimum number of spam comments" is simple. If someone sends me even one spam comment, I want them blocked.

All the IP addresses of blocked Spam comments will now appear further down this screen in the **Spammer IP Address Results** table.

Save your settings before moving on.

The final tabs on the **Spam Prevention** settings are only useful for those using BuddyPress or BBPress. If these scripts are running, the options can add a captcha to their registration form. Since I don't have either script running, there's nothing to see here.

Chapter 20 – Scanner

When a hacker breaks into your site, they'll usually change one or more files on your server. A typical hack would involve injecting malicious code into these files. If successful, they can then use your site for their evil purposes.

Auto email notifications are a great way to catch hackers early on if any files on your server change unexpectedly. In general, WordPress core files, plugin files, and theme files don't change too often. PHP files and JavaScript files are the prime targets of most hackers.

Our plugin can monitor these files and notify you right away if something changes. You'll know if it was you who made the changes the last time you were in your Dashboard. If not, it'll be something or someone more sinister.

The first step to monitoring files is to carry out an initial scan. The plugin can then compare files in the future based on the scan date. At the top of the options screen, click **Perform Scan Now** in the **Manual File Change Detection Scan**.

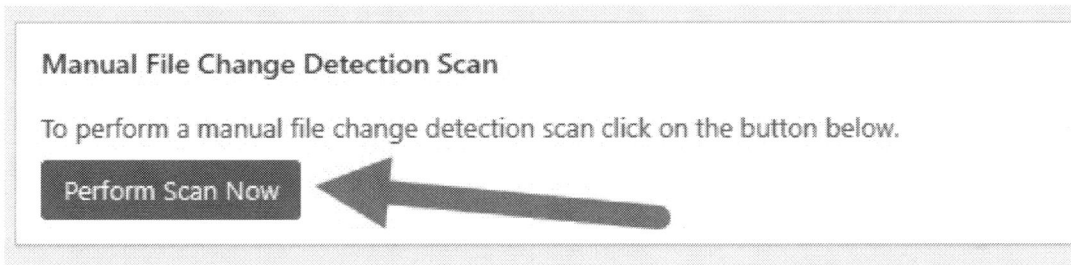

Under the manual scan is a button that allows you to see files that have changed since the last scan. There won't be anything to see yet as we're just setting it up.

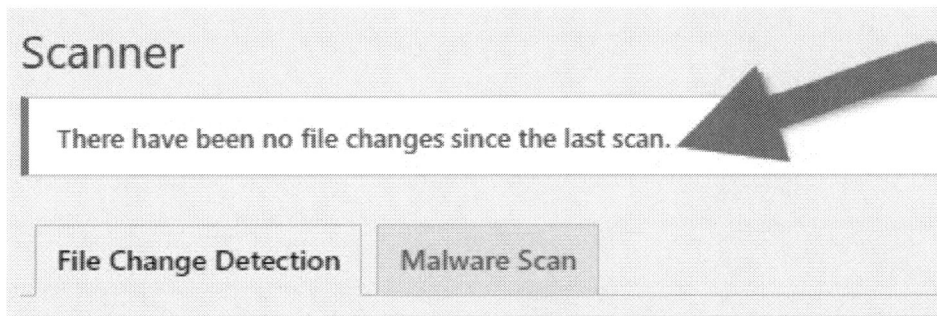

The next panel on this screen is the real workhorse. It carries out automated checks at predefined intervals. This is an "Intermediate" feature, though. Only activate it once you know your basic protection is working fine.

When you're ready, check the **Enable Automated File Change Detection Scan** box.

The default scan frequency is four weeks. The interval you choose determines how long hackers have before the system notifies you. A scan interval of four weeks means it could be four weeks before you find out about any changes.

Note that these scans do take up server resources. Therefore, don't do anything like scan every hour. That's UNLESS you think a hacker is attempting to break into your site, and you want to monitor the situation.

I tend to stick to a 2 – 4-week scan interval on my sites.

You can also set the scan up to ignore certain file types. For example, if you post a lot of images, it's wise to ignore the image file formats you use:

File Types To Ignore:

```
jpg
png
bmp
```

Enter each file type or extension on a new line which you wish detection scan. + More Info

You can get the scan to ignore files or directories as well. If you know where your log files are, or their names, you can exclude those. Similarly, you might want to ignore any caching folder if these are just cached copies of your web pages.

Enter the address you want to use for auto email notifications at the bottom of the screen. Click **Save Changes**.

The **Malware Scan** tab is information about malware and links to tools you can use to scan for malware on your site. There are no settings on this screen.

Chapter 21 – Maintenance

When you want to lock visitors out of your site for any length of time, you can put your site into **Maintenance Mode**. We touched on this earlier when we first looked at the plugin's Dashboard.

The **Maintenance** screen gives you some **Visitor Lockout options.**

The **Enable Front-End Lockout** checkbox will turn maintenance mode on. Visitors will see a message to say that your site is not live right now. The content of the **Enter a Message** box determines the exact message they will see, and you can customize this.

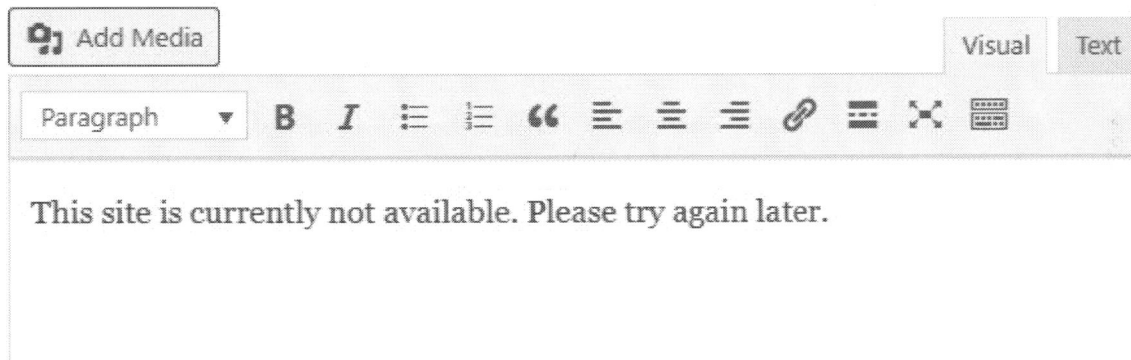

The default message simply states the site is not available and to try again later. You can change this message to read whatever you like. The editor for this is a full WYSIWYG, so you can control the format and even include images, and links, etc.

If you do change the default message, make sure you save the settings before proceeding. Also, make sure you have **Enable Font-end Lockout** DISABLED unless you want it enabled right now.

Chapter 22 – Miscellaneous

The final settings for this plugin are grouped in the **Miscellaneous** screen.

There are four tabs.

The first one is the **Copy Protection tab.** This prevents people from right-clicking on your web pages. It's useful because they can't get the right-click popup menu to inspect (and steal) your web page content. It also stops people from highlighting blocks of text on your page, so it makes copying your content more difficult.

This feature won't stop a determined hacker. It will certainly deter some common thieves, though, who simply want to steal your content.

Check the **Enable Copy Protection** box, and save the settings.

On the **Frames** tab, there is an option to stop other people from putting your web pages into a frame on their website. This type of technique allows them to trick visitors into thinking they're actually on your site. Needless to say, this is a practice that can be quite damaging to you.

To prevent this, check the **Enable iFrame Protection** box, and save settings.

The **Users Enumeration** tab has one option. **Disable Users Enumeration** will prevent hackers (or bots) from accessing useful "hacking info."

Check the box and save the settings.

The final tab is the WP REST API. Since some plugins use the REST API, I recommend you leave this feature disabled.

OK, that's the plugin all set up. Your site is now really well-protected.

Go back and check your Security score. Your results will depend on which features you have activated. Here's how mine looks now:

I've achieved this score after activating all basic and a few "Intermediate" features. Don't worry right now if your score's a lot less. It'll increase as you go in and activate more features over time.

After testing the current security settings, I still have a few other features to activate, so my score will go up.

Notice the above image on the right. When we first began to activate the plugin, that pie chart looked like the one below:

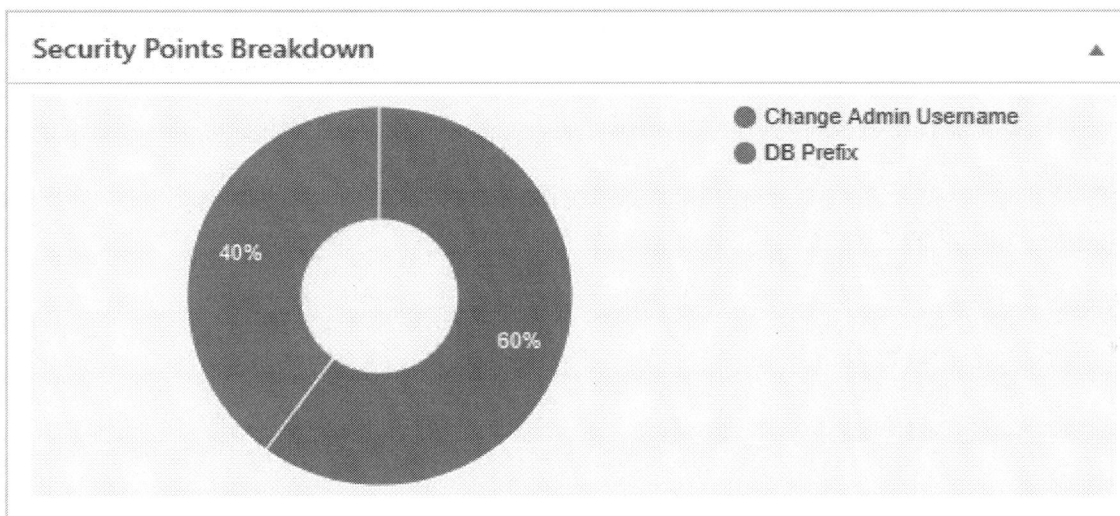

I'm feeling a lot more confident now that my site is secure.

In reality, though, no site is ever 100% safe against the most determined hackers. You probably know this already after seeing the successful hacks of high-profile internet companies. However, the measures you've taken here will keep your site safe against 99.9% of hackers. The ones who could succeed are likely to be more interested in much bigger, higher-profile prey.

And remember, even if the worst did happen — including a server meltdown and your web host not having a backup — it's not the end of the world. You have all the necessary files to restore your site with the backups you've done (and automated) as you went through this book.

In the next chapter, I provide you with a security checklist. This will help you to methodically work your way through as you protect your website(s).

Remember, start with the "**Basic**" features first. Test them for a while before activating the "**Intermediate**" features recommending in this book. Test again for a while, and then go in and tweak some of the "Advanced" options.

Chapter 23 – Security Checklist

This checklist includes items of all the main security fixes you should carry out on your WordPress website. I've included a complete list of those I enable on my sites. If there're any in this list you don't want to implement, just skip them.

The sub-headings refer to the section of the WP security plugin you have to visit to carry out the steps. Some screens have tabs. If I tell you to go to a specific tab, you'll always find it along the top of the screen.

Before you begin to set up the security on a new site, I recommend you scan your site first and do a few backups.

If you want to download this list as a PDF, I have created one you can grab from here: `

https://ezseonews.com/securelist

Initial Tests and Backups

1. Not Included in the Plugin

- ☐ Disable PHP error reporting

2. Scanner Menu

- ☐ On the **File Change Detection** tab, **Perform Scan Now** to check if any files are different from the default installation files. You may find that the .htaccess file has changed, but that's usually fine.
- ☐ Check the option to **Enable Automated File Change Detection Scan**.

3. Settings Menu

- ☐ Backup your Database
- ☐ Backup your .htaccess file
- ☐ Backup your wp-config.php
- ☐ Click on the **WP version Info** tab across the top and check the **Remove WP Generator Meta** box.

Setting up Security

User Accounts Menu

- ☐ On the **WP** Username tab, ensure you are not using **admin** as the username.
- ☐ On the **Display Name** tab, ensure your login name and display name are different.

User Login Menu

- ☐ On the **Login Lockdown** tab, enable **Login Lockdown**.

□ On the **Force Logout** tab, enable the **Force WP User Logout**.

User Registration Menu

□ On the **Manual Approval** tab, enable **Manual approval of new registrations**.
□ On the **Registration Captcha** tab, enable **Captcha on Registration Page**.

Database Security

□ On the **DB Prefix** tab, make sure you're not using the default wp_ as your table prefix.
□ On the **DB Backup** tab, enable automated backups.

Filesystem Security

□ On the **File Permissions** tab, if there are any **Recommended Actions**, take them.
□ On the **PHP File Editing** tab, **Disable the ability to edit PHP Files**.
□ On the **WP File Access** tab, **Prevent Access to WP Default Install Files**.

Firewall

□ On the **Basic Firewall Rules** tab, **Enable Basic Firewall Protection**.
□ If you are not using XMLRPC, you can block it completely; however, I don't recommend this as some plugins will use it.
□ Enable the **Block Access to debug.log file**.
□ On the **Additional Firewall Rules** tab, enable **Disable Index Views**.
□ Enable the **Disable Trace and Track**.
□ Enable **Forbid Proxy Comment Posting**.
□ Enable **Deny Bad Query Strings**.
□ Enable the **Enable Advanced Character String Filter**.
□ On the **6G Blacklist Firewall Rules** tab, check the **Enable 6G Firewall Protection** option.
□ On the **Internet Bots** tab, enable the option to **Block Fake Googlebots**.
□ On the **Prevent Hotlinks** tab, enable the option to **Prevent Image Hotlinking**.
□ On the **404 Detection** tab, check the option to **Enable 404 IP Detection and Lockout**.

Brute Force

□ On the **Cookie Based Brute Force Prevention**, perform the cookie test to make sure your site can use this method of protection. If it can, enter a **Secret** Word and then **Enable Brute Force Attack Prevention** on this tab. If it cannot, go to the **Rename Login Page** tab and use that instead.
□ On the **Login Captcha** tab, enable any of the captchas that you want to use.
□ On the **Honeypot** tab, check the option to **Enable Honeypot on Login Page**.

SPAM Prevention

☐ On the **Comment Spam** tab, check the option to **Enable Captcha On Comment Forms.**

☐ Check the option to **Block Spambots from posting comments.**

☐ On the **Comment SPAM IP Monitoring** tab, check the option to **Enable Auto Block of SPAM Comment IPs.** I recommend you enter a low number into the **Minimum number of SPAM comments** box. I use 1.

Miscellaneous

☐ On the **Copy Protection** tab, check the option to **Enable Copy Protection.**

☐ On the **Frames** tab, check the option to **Enable iFrame Protection.**

☐ On the **Users Enumeration** tab, check the option to **Disable Users Enumeration.**

Chapter 24 – Further Reading

I've included a list of recommended reading for anyone interested in learning more about website security.

I have duplicated the list with clickable links here if you want to view this list in your web browser: https://ezseonews.com/securitylinks

https://www.wordfence.com/blog/2018/04/is-wordpress-secure/

https://en-gb.wordpress.org/about/security/

https://www.wordfence.com/learn/introduction-to-WordPress-security/

https://sucuri.net/guides/wordpress-security/

https://premium.wpmudev.org/blog/keeping-WordPress-secure-the-ultimate-guide/

Where to Go from Here?

I have a couple of resources you may find useful.

YouTube Channel

Lots of video tutorials on using WordPress.

http://ezseonews.com/yt

O.M.G. Facebook Group

A group I initially created for my course students, but I welcome book readers too! Meet, chat, and discuss with other WordPress users. This is an ad-free zone, so you won't be bombarded with people trying to sell you stuff. You will be asked where you heard about the group when you click to join, so just say you are a reader of the book.

http://ezseonews.com/omg

My Site / Newsletter

Find lots of WordPress tutorials. You can sign up for my newsletter while you are there to get notified of new tutorials, books, courses, etc.

https://ezseonews.com/

Useful Resources

There are a few places that I would recommend you visit for more information.

WordPress Tutorials on my Website

https://ezseonews.com/category/wordpress/

My Other Webmaster Books

All my books are available as Kindle books and paperbacks. You can view them all here:

https://amazon.com/author/drandrewwilliams

I'll leave you to explore those if you are interested. You'll find books on various aspects of being a webmaster, such as creating high-quality content, SEO, CSS, etc.

My Video Courses

I have a growing number of video courses hosted on Udemy. You can view a complete list of these at my site:

https://ezseonews.com/udemy

There are courses on the same kinds of topics that my books cover, so SEO, Content Creation, WordPress, Website Analytics, etc.

WordPress Glossary

This glossary lists some of the technical terms I've used in this book. You may also hear these terms when watching other videos or tutorials online. Don't let this list scare you. You do not need to know all of these. This list is for reference only. As you go through this book, if you hear a word you don't understand, look here.

Administrator / Admin - The person that is responsible for maintaining the website, adding pages, etc.

Category Silo - A silo is a closely related group of posts that link to each other but not to less related posts. For example, you might have a category on your site about mountain bikes. All posts in that category are about mountain bikes and link to other articles on mountain bikes. Categories in WordPress allow you to group posts into these silos, so you might hear the term category silo, simply meaning a group of highly related posts, all in the same category.

cPanel - This is your web host control panel that provides an easy-to-use interface and automation tools to simplify your job as site admin.

Child Theme - This is a WordPress theme that inherits its functionality from a parent theme. The parent theme needs to be installed as well as the child theme. Changes made to the child theme won't affect the parent theme so that you can update the parent theme as and when updates are available without trashing your site.

CSS - The layout and design of a web page and its contents are controlled by CSS. This stands for Cascading Style Sheets. You can change colors, font size, alignment of text or images, etc., all using CSS.

Database - A database is a file that contains information. WordPress stores your site content and settings in the database.

Dashboard - This is the WordPress control panel, where you log in to add/edit your website.

Directory (or folder) - You organize files on your computer into folders (also called directories). Web Servers are just computers, and files are organized into directories (or folders) on servers as well.

DNS - DNS stands for Domain Name System. It's a system that converts domain names into numeric IP addresses. See also, Registrar and web host.

Domain / Domain Name - This is your website's web address. e.g., mydomain.com

FTP - Stands for File Transfer Protocol. This is a system for connecting to your webspace so you can add, edit, delete files, etc. Using a tool called an FTP client, you can view all files and folders on your server in much the same way you can with a File Explorer on your computer.

.htaccess - This is a file that is processed by your web server before your web page is loaded in a web browser. You can add specific messages to this file, e.g., to prevent certain people from accessing your site or redirecting an old URL to a new URL.

Host - See Web Host

HTTPS - HTTP defines how content is formatted and transmitted around the web as well as how web servers react to that content. HTTPS is the same as HTTP but uses SSL to ensure content is encrypted.

IP address - This is a unique string of numbers and full stops (periods) that uniquely identify a computer on the internet.

MySQL - This is an open-source database that is commonly used with WordPress installations as well as other web applications.

Plugins - Plugins are pieces of software that can "plugin" to WordPress to add new features. e.g., a plugin might allow you to create a contact form or backup your database on a schedule.

Protocol - Essentially, a set of rules that define how something works.

Registrar - Also called the domain registrar. This is the company that registers your domain for you. They will renew it if you want to. When someone comes to your website, the registrar will send them to your web host via the DNS settings at the registrar. Each web host has a unique DNS, so the visitor will be sent to your web host, where your WordPress site is installed.

Responsive Theme - These themes adjust to the size of the web browser. If someone is viewing your site on a mobile phone, the responsive theme makes sure it looks great. The same site in a desktop browser will also look great as the responsive theme adjusts the layout accordingly.

Root folder - This is the top-level folder on your server where a website is installed. On your home computer, the root folder for any application you have installed will be the folder that contains all the files and sub-folders for that application.

RSS Feed - Stands for Rich Site Summary or Really Simple Syndication. It is a file that contains details of the last X posts on your website. Each post will have details of title, date, description, etc.

SEO - Stands for Search Engine Optimization and refers to the methods you use to try to get your site to rank higher in the search engines.

Shortcodes - A WordPress-specific code that you can use to insert something into a website. E.g., a contact form plugin may give you a shortcode like [cf-form-1]. When the page is rendered in the browser, the shortcode is replaced by the contact form.

SSL - Stands for Secure Sockets Layer. It's a security measure to ensure a connection between two computers is encrypted.

Themes - These are the "skins" of your site. They control the fonts, colors & layout of your site. You can change the look and feel of your site by changing the theme. It takes seconds to do.

URL - the web address you type into your web browser.

Web Host - This is the company that rents you disk space on their computers (servers). You can use that disk space to install your website. When someone visits your website, it's delivered from that web host. The web host has a unique DNS that you give to your registrar.

Webmaster - Same as administrator.

wp-config.php - This file contains the basic setup information for your WordPress site, like database name and other database settings.

Widgets - These are plug-and-play pieces of software that can add features to various areas of your website. e.g., there is a widget that displays a calendar, and this could be placed in the sidebar.

Please Leave a Review/Thought on Amazon

If you enjoyed this book, or even if you didn't, I'd love to hear your comments about it. You can leave your thoughts on the Amazon website.

Printed in Great Britain
by Amazon